Gift to: **Battle for the Bay**

Donald H. Northrop
from
Joshua M. Smith, Speaker
Freeport Historical Society,
Sunday, May 6, 2012, 1:30 PM

The New Brunswick Military Heritage Series, Volume 17

◼ Battle for the Bay

THE NAVAL WAR OF 1812

Joshua M. Smith

**GOOSE LANE EDITIONS and
THE NEW BRUNSWICK MILITARY HERITAGE PROJECT**

Edited by Brent Wilson and Barry Norris.
Front cover illustrations by (top) John Augustus Atkinson, "British Sailors Boarding a Man of War," collection of National Maritime Museum; (bottom) Irwin John Bevan, "Boats of the Maidstone capture the Commodore Barry," collection of the Mariners Museum 1940.0474.000001. Back cover illustrations (top) courtesy of National Archives of Canada; (middle) "Royal Marine, Period 1835," courtesy of the New York Public Library 1199102; and (bottom) courtesy of the Hare family.
Cover and interior page design by Jaye Haworth.
Art direction by Julie Scriver.
Printed in Canada.
10 9 8 7 6 5 4 3 2 1

Library and Archives Canada Cataloguing in Publication

Smith, Joshua M. (Joshua Mitchell)
    Battle for the Bay: the Naval War of 1812 / Joshua M. Smith.

(New Brunswick military heritage series; 17)
Co-published by: Gregg Centre for the Study of War and Society.
Includes bibliographical references and index.
ISBN 978-0-86492-644-9

1. Canada — History — War of 1812 — Naval operations. 2. United States — History — War of 1812 — Naval operations. 3. Fundy, Bay of — History, Military. 4. Maine, Gulf of — History, Military. I. Gregg Centre for the Study of War and Society II. Title. III. Series: New Brunswick military heritage series; 17

FC449.N3S55 2010   971.03'4   C2010-907060-7

Goose Lane Editions acknowledges the financial support of the Canada Council for the Arts, the government of Canada through the Canada Book Fund (CBF), and the government of New Brunswick through the Department of Wellness, Culture and Sport.

Goose Lane Editions
Suite 330, 500 Beaverbrook Court
Fredericton, New Brunswick
CANADA E3B 5X4
www.gooselane.com

New Brunswick Military Heritage Project
The Brigadier Milton F. Gregg, VC
Centre for the Study of War and Society
University of New Brunswick
PO Box 4400
Fredericton, New Brunswick
CANADA E3B 5A3
www.unb.ca/nbmhp

FSC
Mixed Sources
Cert no. SW-COC-000952
© 1996 FSC

To Scott See,
who introduced me to Canadian history.

Contents

9   **Introduction**

13   **Chapter One** Nelson Is Gone: Constabulary Duties, 1783-1812

31   **Chapter Two** "For the Service of the Province": The Provincial Sloop *Brunswicker* and Littoral Defence

55   **Chapter Three** *Bream* Brings the War to the Enemy

75   **Chapter Four** "The Sea-Fight Far Away": H.M. Brig *Boxer* and the Fog of War

93   **Epilogue**

103   **Conclusion** Après la guerre

105   **Appendix Table 1** Prizes Captured by H.M. Schooner *Bream*, 1812-1813

107   **Appendix Table 2** Inventory of Items Sold from H.M. Brig *Boxer*, November 1813

109   **Acknowledgements**

111   **Selected Bibliography**

115   **Photo Credits**

117   **Index**

Introduction

Writing on board his ship H.M.S. *Blenheim* in 1839, Captain Sir Henry Le Fleming Senhouse of the Royal Navy looked back to his time as commodore of the British naval forces in the Bay of Fundy during the War of 1812. Sir Henry was writing an endorsement for his friend Lieutenant Charles Hare, whose "activity and enterprize" in destroying US coastal trade and privateers won the admiration of Senhouse "and of every officer who knew him." Yet, notwithstanding Hare's undeniable ability, Senhouse had to admit that Hare's case was one of "neglected merit," for the unfortunate officer had remained at the rank of lieutenant for thirty-seven years despite his performance during the last war with the Americans. Hare's lack of recognition parallels that of the naval War of 1812 as it played out in the battle for the Bay of Fundy. This work aims to rescue the service of Hare and his fellow Royal Navy officers and sailors from obscurity by examining three warships that played important roles in defending New Brunswick.

These vessels, the provincial sloop *Brunswicker*, His Majesty's schooner *Bream*, and His Majesty's brig-of-war *Boxer*, were small and operated out of Saint John during the war. While many Canadians are aware of the naval battles fought on the Great Lakes or the frigate duels fought on the ocean during the War of 1812, few will know of the naval component as it relates to the Maritimes, except for those who might recall it had something to do with privateers. The vessels that fought this war were small, yet extremely busy, and often involved in low-level combat against various US forces.

The size of these vessels and the missions assigned to them indicate that they were not warships designed to engage with enemy fleets in grand battles, but patrol craft. In peacetime they performed a constabulary role, enforcing maritime law and policy. In wartime they engaged in a form of naval warfare known as *guerre de course* that emphasized attacking the enemy's commercial shipping and protecting one's own. It was not the sort of glamorous duty that made for rapid promotion, as Lieutenant Hare found to his dismay. But it was important work, even if it was tedious to fight winter winds, summer fogs, and the fierce tidal currents of the notoriously dangerous Bay of Fundy. It could also be deadly: shipwreck, combat, and imprisonment were constant hazards.

The Bay of Fundy and the Gulf of Maine generally is an area that has been largely ignored in histories of the War of 1812. The frequent small-scale combat fought in these waters between privateers and government vessels has received little consideration. In part this is because of the historiographical "big ship" bias that emphasizes blue-water battles. The War of 1812 in the Bay of Fundy and off the New England coast was decidedly not a big-ship conflict; privateers, from both the United States and the Maritime colonies, usually were less than one hundred tons and some were mere open rowboats. The naval units were equally rudimentary: a few sloops-of-war, gun brigs, and schooners. This was a petty raiding war, *guerre de course* in a littoral, or coastal, environment. Although they seldom operated together as a squadron, let alone a fleet, these naval forces nevertheless played an important role in the war, convoying ships between ports, patrolling the bay for hostile vessels, and raiding the enemy's coast.

"View of Province Hall and public offices, Fredericton, New Brunswick" by George Neilson Smith. PANB Isaac Erb Fonds: P11-57

Chapter One

Nelson Is Gone:
Constabulary Duties, 1783-1812

Early in January 1806, the news of Admiral Horatio Nelson's great victory at Trafalgar reached New Brunswick. It was an era of national pride for the British Empire, its monarchy, and the Royal Navy, and thus the response was both public and unrestrained. For years, New Brunswickers had been following the exploits of Nelson, the first of Britain's truly national heroes. News of his victory over a French fleet off Egypt in 1798, for example, was met with spontaneous celebrations. Flags flew from Saint John's fortifications and ships in the harbour, and cannon salutes were fired. The wealthy illuminated their windows with candles, a festive manner of celebrating their patriotism. New Brunswickers greeted the news of Trafalgar with a similar response. Accounts of the battle were published in full in the province's newspapers. Many of the better off celebrated the victory by again placing candles in each window. A ball was held in Saint John in honour of the event, attended by a "great assembly of beauty and fashion." There were public dinners and the drinking of many loyal toasts throughout the province.

The most elaborate celebration was an all-night ball held in the Province Hall in Fredericton. The decorations featured patriotic themes, and after supper loyal toasts were made, interspersed with patriotic songs such as "Rule Britannia." A song was also composed in honour of the late victory of the "immortal Nelson":

To The Memory of Lord Nelson

Though envied and hated by Tyrants and Slaves,
Britannia, fair Queen of the Ocean, remains:
Repell'd by her ramparts that float on the waves,
War flies from her borders and want from her plains.
For ages renown'd,
By Victory crown'd,
Surpassed by no other,
One rivals his brother,
And all prove their titles as Lords of the Main.
Lords of the Main? Aye, Lords of the Main,
The Tars of Old England are Lords of the Main.
The Charter descending from heroes of old,
Expands in succession, as ages roll on,
A climax of glory; but ah, can it hold?
Who shall rival the past, now that *Nelson is gone;*
Yet hark, from on high
The Angelic reply.
Your Nelson shall conquer and triumph again.
Each Tar shall inherit
A share of his spirit,
And all prove invincible Lords of the Main.
Lords of the Main? Aye, Lords of the Main,
The Tars of Old England are Lords of the Main.
Wherever your far-dreaded sails are unfurl'd,
The genius of Nelson shall fight by your side,
And teach you again to astonish the world
By deeds unexampled, achievements untried.
Then Britons strike home,
For ages to come

Your Nelson shall conquer and triumph again.
Each Tar shall inherit
A share of his spirit,
And all prove invincible Lords of the Main.
Lords of the Main? Aye, Lords of the Main,
The Tars of Old England are Lords of the Main.
Nor are we alone in the noble career,
The Soldier partakes of the generous flame;
To glory he marches, to glory we steer,
Between us we share the rich harvest of fame.
Recorded on high,
Their names never die,
Whose deeds the renown of their Country sustain.
The King, then, God bless him,
The world shall confess him,
The Lord of those men who are Lords of the Main.
Lords of the Main? Aye, Lords of the Main.
The Tars of Old England are Lords of the Main.

Perhaps not a memorable song, but reflective of the spirit of the age known as the Regency period, described so brilliantly in the literature of Jane Austen. Indeed, Jane Austen's brother Charles served as commander of H.M. sloop-of-war *Indian* on the North American station, a ship that often visited the Bay of Fundy. Effusive patriotism was in fashion during this period, and New Brunswickers were no exception. Hoisting a cup to numerous toasts, singing and composing songs, and dancing until dawn were all joyful means to celebrate the colony's connection to the largest, wealthiest, most powerful empire on the planet, and, as they understood it, the one that offered the greatest degree of liberty. New Brunswickers revelled in its naval triumphs, and named places after Nelson and Trafalgar, especially in the port city of Saint John. Some New Brunswickers had even taken part in the battle; one was young William Carleton, son of the colony's first governor, who served as a midshipman on H.M.S. *Colossus*. The colony's greatest contribution to victory at Trafalgar, however, was not its native sons but its trees: the ships of Admiral Nelson's fleet were built with masts from New Brunswick's virgin forest that had been floated down the St. John River and loaded onto specialized ships that carried them to Britain's great naval bases.

Yet the colony's relationship to the mighty Royal Navy is not easy to discern. New Brunswick had no permanent naval facility; warships visited it only from time to time, and even then they were not always a welcome presence. While Loyalist families eagerly sought commissions in the army for their sons, they were less likely to find a midshipman's berth in the Royal Navy. Understanding this complex relationship requires a brief understanding of New Brunswick's place within the British Empire, the constabulary role of the Royal Navy in the Bay of Fundy, and the twin problems of naval impressment and desertion.

Britain's Maritime Empire

In 1806, the British Empire stretched from the wilds of Upper Canada to the penal settlements of Australia. It was primarily a maritime empire, joined by the bonds of seaborne commerce and the might of the Royal Navy, the largest and most effective naval force the world had ever seen. With Nelson's victory at Trafalgar, Britain's dominance of the seas seemed assured: its merchant and naval fleets truly ruled the waves. The Royal Navy alone had about one hundred ships of the line, seven hundred other vessels, and about 145,000 personnel afloat. What remained of the French fleet occasionally broke out of the rigorous blockade the Royal Navy imposed, but it offered no real threat. The navy dismantled the fleets of other potential opponents, such as the Danes, by seizing and carrying them away to Britain.

New Brunswick's role in this mighty maritime empire was threefold: as a Loyalist refuge, link to Lower Canada, and supplier of mast timber. The British government had created the colony of New Brunswick in 1784 as a refuge for Loyalists fleeing the United States at the end of the American Revolution. From the time the Loyalists stepped ashore, the Royal Navy was a presence, offering protection from US encroachment and enforcing imperial trade regulations. New Brunswick also provided the only means of communication to Lower Canada during the winter, when the St. Lawrence River was frozen. Since Saint John was ice free, messengers could land there year-round and proceed up the St. John River past Fredericton and the Madawaska area to Quebec and then on to Upper Canada. Ultimately, this route would be used to send reinforcements, including Royal Navy seamen, to Upper and Lower Canada during the War of 1812.

Finally, New Brunswick provided an important supply of a relatively rare and highly valuable resource that helped hold the empire together: ships' masts, for both commercial purposes and the Royal Navy. In 1784, the Admiralty established a mast and spar reserve in Charlotte County between St. Stephen and St. George, and began cutting its huge white pines in 1796. It is estimated that the colony's masts cost only half as much as those from the Baltic Sea region and were less vulnerable to interdiction or trade restrictions. Mast ships departing Saint John and St. Andrews were large vessels of over seven hundred tons, valuable enough to merit convoy protection from the Bay of Fundy to Halifax, Britain, or the Caribbean — the mast ship *Minerva*, for example, warranted the protection of the frigate H.M.S. *Boston* on its voyage to the West Indies in December 1800. The colony's mast production peaked in 1811 at just over three thousand sticks. It was a lucrative trade for some.

New Brunswick generally had a military garrison but it was never intended to have a naval base. Instead, Halifax was the headquarters of the British North American fleet, but it was a sleepy little naval station. Even with the outbreak of war between Britain and France in 1793, the ships based in Halifax saw little action. French warships were seldom encountered. The admiral stationed there often dispatched small vessels to patrol New Brunswick's waters, but never one larger than a frigate. These patrols performed policing or constabulary duties, such as chasing American fishermen out of British-controlled waters and attempting to stop the extensive smuggling between the Maritime colonies and the United States. As early as 1784, Royal Navy vessels patrolled the Bay of Fundy to enforce Governor Thomas Carleton's prohibition of commercial intercourse with the Americans.

Overall, however, the Royal Navy's role in suppressing smuggling was neither significant nor enthusiastic. Its greatest impact was more indirect: if a British naval vessel was nearby both US citizens and British subjects stayed off the water for fear of being impressed into the Royal Navy. But Royal Navy officers were not eager to pursue smugglers. They disliked cooperating with customs officials, let alone taking orders from them, and they knew that litigious colonial ship owners were likely to sue them in courts that favoured local influence over imperial regulation. Even the colonial Vice-Admiralty Courts, whose judges were sent out from Britain, were not very supportive of Royal Navy seizures, condemning only about one-quarter of the craft seized by the navy for smuggling. Clearly, a young commander could get himself into a great deal of trouble chasing smugglers, and he was not likely to profit from zealously enforcing commercial laws. Nonetheless, when New Brunswick's military administrator asked in July 1811 for the navy's help in suppressing smuggling in the Bay of Fundy, the region's naval commander complied. Admiral Warren sent the small schooner *Cuttle* to patrol the area to stop smugglers and recruit seamen. *Cuttle* had some success when she seized the Nova Scotia schooner *Boyne* and a Nantucket vessel, but such small seizures barely put a dent into the smuggling trade.

What naval officers really wanted to do was to fight the French. On occasion, French vessels did appear in the Bay of Fundy, but the Royal Navy was often engaged elsewhere, so locals had to fall back on their own resources to defend their coast and shipping. In September 1795, the French privateer *La Solide* captured several vessels out of Saint John. With no Royal Navy vessels in the area, inhabitants, alarmed by the prospect of "some predatory enterprize on shore," particularly at St. Andrews, begged Governor Carleton for protection. He responded by chartering the armed brig *Union* for three months to patrol the Bay of Fundy. Eventually, H.M.S. *Lynx* arrived, tracked down the raider, and captured it near Campobello Island. With assurances from the admiral in Halifax that he would send a ship to protect the bay, Carleton dismissed the brig. When, in August 1801, another French privateer, *L'Espiral*, entered the Bay of Fundy and seized two vessels, the people of Saint John, rather

Halifax, British North America's most important
naval base during the War of 1812. NAC

than relying on the Royal Navy to protect them, fitted out the armed brig
Discovery and set off in pursuit. A small naval vessel belatedly showed
up to join the chase, but the French ship evaded all efforts to find it and
got away. After the battle at Trafalgar in 1805, French ships never again
threatened the Bay of Fundy. But a new potential opponent much closer
to New Brunswick was rising to challenge Britain: the United States.

Impressment

The Royal Navy always had difficulty manning its ships during wartime.
Some sailors volunteered for service, but the number fell far short of the
requirements of the expanded wartime fleet. As a result, the navy fell
back on the practice of impressment, forcibly taking seamen from ships
at sea or while in port and compelling them to serve on its warships.
Once a man had been seized by the press gang, he was offered a choice:
either sign up as a volunteer and receive the benefits that came with that
status, such as a substantial cash bonus, shore leave, or promotion to
petty officer, or remain a "pressed man" and receive nothing. Volunteers

British impressment of American sailors was a main cause of the War of 1812. Florida Center for Institutional Technology

were considered more effective than pressed men. It was often said that, "Better one volunteer than three pressed men." Seamen in Halifax and other ports were lured to sign up with hearty advertisements such as this one, dated May 21, 1813:

> What should Sailors do on Shore,
> While King, Country and Fortune point to the Ocean!
> His Majesty's Schooner *PICTOU*, of 12 guns, commanded
> by Lieut. Stephens, as fine a vessel of her size as ever
> floated on salt water, wants a few jolly, spirited fellows to
> complete her complement for a short cruise... Apply on
> board, at the Navy Yard.

Years later, New Brunswick-born poet Bliss Carman also explored naval recruiting through his poem, "A Captain of the Press Gang," published in 1894. Carman, a master at creating scenes and moods, deftly captures the blandishments of a recruiting officer trying to convince seamen to leave their shoreside haunts and return to sea:

> I've aboard a hundred messmates
> Better than these 'long-shore knaves.
> There is wreckage on the shallows;
> 'Tis the open sea that saves.

> Hark, lad, dost not hear it calling?
> That's the voice thy father knew,
> When he took the King's good cutlass
> In his grip, and fought it through.

> Who would palter at press-money
> When he heard that sea-cry vast?
> That's the call makes lords of lubbers,
> When they ship before the mast.

Royal Navy historian N.A.M. Rodger believes that impressment was a pretty humdrum affair on the whole, with sailors by and large accepting their fate, while Canadian historians such as Keith Mercer have attempted to establish crowd violence associated with press gangs as a sort of proto-Canadian nationalism. Rodger has much the better of the argument, as British North Americans took little notice of the practice in general, especially if it took place on board ships, even when anchored in port. Certainly, the Royal Navy personnel involved took little notice, simply entering into their logbooks how many sailors were impressed in a given day.

Impressment was a complex issue because not only did colonial seamen resent the practice, but the Royal Navy, despite protests by the US government, also seized sailors from US ships, which often included in their crews British seamen and Royal Navy deserters attracted by the high wages offered by US shipowners. The people of the Maritime colonies, their region suffering from a chronic shortage of labourers, made the situation worse by urging sailors to desert — farmers, fishermen, and timber merchants were as anxious for working hands as the navy was. And because service in the Royal Navy was harsh, sailors needed little prompting to desert. Accordingly, authorities attempting to apprehend deserters received little local help. In 1813, New Brunswick's Assembly resisted an attempt to pass legislation that would have empowered officials chasing deserters to enter any dwelling or building despite the objections of its owners.

The press gang was a problem throughout British North America. As a major naval base, Halifax witnessed widespread impressment, and in 1805 a major riot occurred in response to a press gang that killed one man and injured seven others. In 1807, a man was shot dead attempting to flee impressment near Quebec City. Lower Canada's merchants had long opposed the practice because ships working through the intricate channels of the St. Lawrence River were more likely to be wrecked if they were undermanned.

In New Brunswick, the press gang usually operated in Saint John or Passamaquoddy Bay. In August 1809, for example, Lieutenant William

Royal Navy sailor ashore.

Frissell, commanding H.M. gun brig *Plumper*, impressed George Laighton from the schooner *Fairplay* as it lay at Saint John harbour. Laighton then sued for release, a common practice for impressed sailors, and one that often worked. One Saturday night in the summer of 1813, a press gang led by Master's Mate James Hugh of H.M. brig *Boxer* broke into the second floor bedroom of William Shives as he was preparing for bed and beat him.

But New Brunswickers were more likely to respond by concealing themselves. When local seafarers learned that a Royal Navy vessel was nearby, they would not venture out on the water or into the streets for fear of being impressed. This, however, could immobilize the colony's valuable timber trade. According to scholar Julian Gwyn, even the valuable mast ships encountered problems procuring crew unless they secured special protection from impressment. On several occasions, the presence of British warships in Passamaquoddy Bay kept Charlotte County fishermen and other seafarers off the bay for weeks, interrupting the local economy.

Nevertheless, despite colonial and US protests, Royal Navy vessels continued to impress sailors until the end of the Napoleonic Wars. Indeed, British warships impressed American seamen right up until the US Congress declared war on Britain. As late as April 28, 1812, H.M. schooner *Chubb* impressed a Yankee seaman while on a cruise from Saint John, despite his producing documents establishing his nationality. So it was no surprise, then, that impressment was a major reason President James Madison asked Congress to declare war in June 1812.

Jefferson's Embargo

Conflict between Britain and the United States over the issue of impressment first came to a head in 1807 around the *Chesapeake* incident. The frigate U.S.S. *Chesapeake* had enlisted several deserters from the Royal Navy, a fact known and resented by British naval officers. In June 1807, the *Chesapeake* left Norfolk, Virginia, destined for the Mediterranean. A larger British warship, H.M.S. *Leopard*, intercepted the *Chesapeake* and demanded to search the US warship for British deserters. When the American commander refused, *Leopard* fired into the Yankee frigate and quickly overwhelmed it. A boarding party then went aboard and removed four deserters. The US ship limped back to port, where the American public responded with great anger to the attack. President Thomas Jefferson ordered all British warships out of US waters, and it appeared that Britain and the United States would go to war.

These tensions were reflected in a small way in New Brunswick. About the same time as the *Chesapeake* incident, the small British naval schooner *Porgey* sailed into Passamaquoddy Bay and fired its cannon, seized US ships, impressed Britons and Americans indiscriminately, and beat mariners who resisted. American officials sent alarmed reports to Washington, further fuelling US anger with Britain.

Neither side was ready for war, however, or really wanted it. Jefferson, knowing that the United States was completely unprepared, instead chose to use an embargo to punish the British for harassing US shipping. Under this policy, theoretically, no US ship was allowed to leave port for foreign markets, nor were foreign ships allowed to take cargoes away from the United States. The embargo could have devastated colonies such as New Brunswick, which relied on US flour and foodstuffs. But that potential was never realized because Americans quickly learned how profitable it was to violate the embargo by selling flour to British subjects.

New Brunswickers, in any case, were not eager for war. Activating the militia in the winter of 1808 nearly bankrupted the colony, and Saint John's commercial community knew it was wiser to profit by subverting the embargo than to suffer from outright war with troublesome US neighbours. Undermining the embargo by smuggling became the call of the hour; one could even claim it was patriotic because it helped feed hungry mouths in British North America.

One of the most popular and convenient places to engage in this illicit trade was Passamaquoddy Bay, on the colony's western boundary. US merchants could bring flour and other products legally to Eastport, Maine, and then arrange to smuggle it across the border at night or through the thick fogs that frequently enveloped the bay's waters. British imperial officials, too, were eager to blunt the impact of the embargo, and permitted and even encouraged the flour smugglers, resulting in a roaring trade in flour at 'Quoddy that ensured a plentiful supply for the Maritime colonies and even British military and naval units stationed in the region. Eventually, the United States sent soldiers and naval vessels to patrol the border area. Britain responded by sending H.M. sloop-of-war *Squirrel* and other vessels to defend its territory from the US Navy's overzealous pursuit of flour smugglers.

The Royal Navy's intervention proved effective, even crucial, to the smuggling trade that subverted the embargo. US officials at Passamaquoddy raged that they could see the decks of British warships stacked high with smuggled flour. Royal Navy vessels such as the brig *Plumper* even escorted ships loaded with flour out of the bay to ensure that US patrol craft would not interfere with them. When US naval vessels did seize British ships and their contraband cargoes, merchants

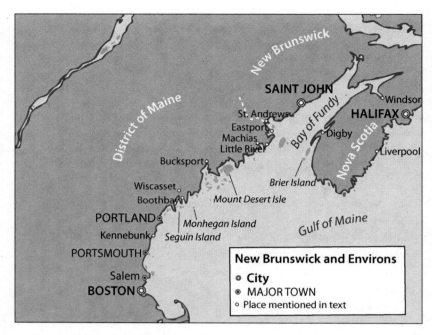

The Gulf of Maine and the Bay of Fundy region, where the Royal Navy's primary role was that of a maritime constabulary. Note: At the time of the War of 1812, the District of Maine was a part of Massachusetts; Maine attained statehood in 1820. Joshua M. Smith

quickly appealed to Royal Navy officers for protection. On one occasion, when a Yankee gunboat seized a British ship loaded with flour and a Royal Navy officer demanded its return, the gunboat's officer replied that "nothing but bloodshed and hard fighting" would get it back. Happily, cooler heads prevailed, and the young American officer returned the ship to its owners.

Jefferson's embargo ultimately proved unenforceable and collapsed before Congress repealed it in early 1809. A number of lesser trade restrictions continued, however, and New Brunswick became a convenient base for illicit trade with the United States. This smuggling did little to ease tensions between the United States and Britain, but it revived New

Brunswick's maritime economy. New Brunswick's agent in London was so pleased with the embargo's effect that he even went so far as to "applaud Jefferson very much as an Englishman, and especially as a New Brunswick agent and planter." The story was less happy for the deserters removed from the *Chesapeake*. They were court-martialled in Halifax and all found guilty. One was sentenced to death and was hanged from the yardarm of the sloop *Halifax*. The other three, in light of their former good conduct and professed contrition, were sentenced to be flogged around the fleet at Halifax, receiving five hundred lashes each. As it turned out, more sailors would be executed and flogged at Halifax for an attempted mutiny in New Brunswick waters.

Mutiny and Desertion in the Bay of Fundy
Desertion went hand in hand with impressment, and to counter the Maritime population's sympathy with seamen attempting to escape Royal Navy service, colonial legislatures outlawed the harbouring of deserters and paid rewards for returning them, but to little effect. Americans at Passamaquoddy also encouraged sailors to desert, and in the summer of 1809 they nearly incited a successful mutiny on H.M. sloop-of-war *Columbine* as it lay at anchor between Campobello, New Brunswick, and Eastport, Maine.

The reasons for the mutiny are various. In part, it was because the ship's sailors knew they could make good money on Yankee merchant ships, but *Columbine*'s commander, Captain George Hills, was also notorious for having his men flogged for the least offence. Nova Scotian scholar Martin Hubley theorizes that the large number of US and Irish sailors in particular among *Columbine*'s crew did not identify with their officers.

Problems began on July 4. While Americans gathered at Eastport to toast and salute Independence Day with artillery, six of *Columbine*'s crew made their own bid for liberty, four scampering off in St. Andrews and two others in a separate incident. That night, there was a further desertion, with thirteen seamen and three marines taking the vessel's jolly boat. Captain Hills attempted to make up for the loss of crew by impressing fourteen sailors out of merchant vessels anchored at St. Andrews. A few days later, however, another seven seamen successfully deserted, and Hills had to discharge two of the impressed men as unsuitable for service. Most frustrating of all for the captain was that many of the deserters had taken refuge just a few hundred yards away in Eastport, under US jurisdiction.

Columbine was still short of sailors, and Hills had been forced to put some of the crew in irons. It seemed likely that many would be flogged severely for attempting to desert. The crew grumbled, complained even about ordinary duties, and said they were treated like "slaves." Slowly, they developed a plot to seize the ship and murder the officers. Tensions were high, and the officers sensed that all was not right. On the night of August 1, tipped off by an informer, Hills moved to arrest the ringleaders. A scuffle broke out, the captain intervened and shot the chief mutineer himself. The captain then called for assistance from the New Brunswick militia to help guard against further trouble while he got the vessel to the safety of Saint John. When *Columbine* later reached Halifax, a Royal Navy court martial tried twenty-three of her crew. A number were ordered to be flogged through the squadron, and others were flogged and then transported to Australia in irons. Six more were hanged; four of the corpses were left hanging from gibbets at Maugher's Beach in Halifax as a public warning that the authority of the Royal Navy was not to be taken lightly. Nonetheless, desertion continued to be a problem for British forces in and around the Bay of Fundy.

Conclusion

New Brunswickers had a complex relationship with the Royal Navy. While the navy undoubtedly protected trade, it also could be a troublesome presence. A few Saint John merchants made fortunes from providing masts to the navy, and some families procured berths for their sons as midshipmen. Lesser merchants involved in smuggling, however, resented the navy's sometimes heavy-handed enforcement of trade regulations. The colony's ordinary mariners, fishermen, and sailors often feared impressment as they went about their business. The Royal Navy's constabulary role and its relatively ineffective response to the rare French forays into the Bay of Fundy further contributed to the indifference of

New Brunswickers to the service. That attitude would change dramatic-ally in late spring 1812, however, as war clouds gathered. Soon, New Brunswick would be swept up in the conflict between Britain and the United States, and the Loyalist colony would come to appreciate the Royal Navy as its protector.

Irwin John Bevan's twentieth-century interpretation of the capture of the US revenue cutter *Commodore Barry*. Mariners' Museum QW 280

"For the Service of the Province": The Provincial Sloop *Brunswicker* and Littoral Defence

The June 27, 1812, headline of the New Brunswick *Royal Gazette* could not have been clearer: "WAR! WAR! WAR!" it read, and detailed how the news had arrived from the border. Tremors of war had long been felt in the Loyalist colony. Now that it was here, how would it be conducted? As it turned out, few pitched battles were fought in the Bay of Fundy and adjacent waters; instead, the local experience can best be classified as low-intensity warfare, in which force is applied selectively and with restraint. Along with military force, each side might attempt to subvert the other through economic and political means. A hallmark of low-intensity warfare is the driving of military decisions by political objectives. As the German military philosopher Karl von Clausewitz wrote, "The political object, as the original motive of the war, should be the standard for determining both the aim of the military force and also the amount of effort to be made."

In this instance, both the US and British governments chose to make the Bay of Fundy and the New England coast a secondary theatre and to focus their main efforts elsewhere. Regular units were small, and they exercised restraint to an almost painful degree. For example, the US commander of Fort Sullivan, which overlooked the boundary between Maine and New Brunswick, was forbidden from firing on Royal Navy warships as they passed up Passamaquoddy Bay. The British warships for their part always lowered their colours when passing the battery, making it clear that they did not intend to attack.

In such a low-intensity conflict, acts of magnanimity were as important as acts of violence for the forces involved. Paroling prisoners of war, returning trunks to captured sailors, and even conducting elaborate funerals for fallen enemies were common in the region. The British admiral in charge of the Halifax station, Herbert Sawyer, quickly grasped this concept, and knowing that the New England states were largely opposed to the war, did his utmost to facilitate an illicit trade with willing US merchants and refused to blockade the New England coast. He did not have enough ships on hand to carry the war to the enemy in any case.

The type of war fought in New Brunswick's waters early in the war was also a form of low-level conflict known as *guerre de course* (hunting warfare). In general, the point of *guerre de course* was to capture the enemy's merchant shipping and protect one's own, thereby hindering the enemy's economy and supply chain while defending friendly cargo vessels. It was fought by small naval vessels acting alone, or by privateers — privately owned vessels licensed by government to attack enemy shipping. Irregular units, such as militia or privateersmen, were also a part of this small-scale warfare, but, without major ideological or cultural differences, their primary activities revolved around the acquisition or defence of property and were relatively bloodless.

This *guerre de course* was fought in the littoral, or near-coastal, environment of the Bay of Fundy. It was not just a matter of operating in coastal waters, though; sea forces also came ashore to skirmish, and sometimes land units took to small craft to engage with naval units or privateers. US privateersmen fully embraced the littoral warfare concept in that they were more likely to go ashore in search of plunder, despite its clear illegality. In June 1813, for example, the US privateer *Weasel* raided homes in Beaver Harbour, New Brunswick, taking not only trade goods but also household furniture and even women's and children's clothing. These privateersmen also had few scruples about plundering an American farmer of his chickens one night — perhaps a case of overidentifying with the name of their boat. Charlotte County's militia went in pursuit of the *Weasel* in three boats, chased the Yankees ashore at Grand Manan Island and rescued the stolen property.

As the *Weasel* incident indicates, the vessels involved in this littoral warfare were usually small — sometimes mere open boats, but more often two-masted schooners or brigs, with only the occasional British frigate appearing on the scene. As a rule, the larger the warship, the less time it spent in littoral operations. That said, the bigger vessels tended to create much greater panic among the coastal populace, not so much because of their larger batteries, but because they carried smaller boats or barges with which to comb coastal waters for prizes or launch shore raids.

Yankee Privateers

The most common US units operating in the Bay of Fundy were privateers from ports such as Gloucester or Salem, Massachusetts. While the owners and officers of these vessels saw the war as an opportunity to make money, they also tended to have ideological motivations based on their adherence to Jeffersonian ideals of equality, territorial aggrandizement, and a dislike of all things British. Ill-disciplined amateurs, they often violated the magnanimous approach regular military and naval officers displayed. Many such privateers immediately sailed for the approaches to the Bay of Fundy on hearing the news of the declaration of war. Their goal was to capture British and colonial shipping coming out of St. Andrews and Saint John.

A typical example of the Yankee privateers that harassed New Brunswick shipping was the chebacco boat[1] *Fame*, a modern replica of which currently operates as a commercial charter vessel. The replica's captain, Michael Rutstein, author of a thoroughly researched and very accessible book about the original's career entitled *Fame: The Salem Privateer*, concludes that the twenty-five men who joined together to man

---

1   Chebacco was a small port in Essex County, Massachusetts, whose fishermen, sometime around the American Revolution, developed a two-masted vessel with a schooner rig for the inshore fisheries. The design was simple and practical, and soon found favour throughout coastal northern New England.

Salem privateers such as the *Fame* captured many vessels sailing out of Saint John. Captain Michael Rutstein, http://www.schoonerfame.com

the *Fame* in 1812 were modest sea captains, merchants, and shipowners who could not afford to be without work but were not rich enough to invest in privateers while remaining safely at home. When war appeared imminent, they pooled their resources to purchase a fast, recently built fishing schooner. The *Fame* was about fifty feet long with a broad bow and a pointed "pink" stern;[2] she carried two small cannon and a crew of up to thirty. On July 1, 1812, the owners having received a privateering commission, the *Fame* set sail for her chosen hunting grounds in the

---

2   Chebacco boats often featured a "pink" stern that pinched together, instead of a flat transom or rounded stern.

Bay of Fundy. New Brunswickers had known about the war for less than seventy-two hours. As Rutstein relates,

> It didn't take long for *Fame* to hit the jackpot. In a few
> days she was off Grand Manan, on the border between
> the United States and Canada, and fell in with the ship
> *Concord* of Plymouth, England, and the Scottish brig *Elbe*.
> Both vessels surrendered without firing a shot. *Fame* was
> back in port by July 9th, just eight days after setting out,
> and her prizes arrived a few days later. *Concord*, with her
> cargo of masts, spars, staves, and lumber, and *Elbe* with
> tar, staves and spars, were condemned as legitimate prizes
> and sold at auction. The net proceeds were $4,690.67 —
> nearly ten times what *Fame* had cost!

The problem for New Brunswick was that the *Fame* was but one of many such Yankee privateers that swarmed the Bay of Fundy. The *Fame* herself would venture forth on no less than twelve cruises before being wrecked on the Seal Islands off Nova Scotia in spring 1814.

Privateers mostly were a nuisance rather than a real threat, but in the early days of the war they made some significant captures. For example, the tiny Salem privateer *Madison*, armed with just one cannon, captured a British transport brig bound for Saint John with a cargo of gunpowder, 880 sets of uniforms for the 104th (New Brunswick) Regiment of Foot, and camp equipment and band instruments. In this instance, Britain's loss was America's gain, and the 104th's uniforms clothed drummers and musicians in the US military.

The Royal Navy was stretched thin at the beginning of the war, but its response was rapid, using both convoys and cruising as tactics to engage the enemy's smaller vessels in the Bay of Fundy. Occasionally, larger ships, such as frigates, would attempt to sweep the coast free of troublesome raiders as well, but by and large this was a war conducted by lesser vessels.

Convoys in the Bay of Fundy typically gathered at Saint John and picked up more vessels off Campobello Island. The escorting ships were

Facing page: A convoy signals book, circa 1812; the region's
frequent fogs often rendered the system ineffective.

NARA RG 21, "Records of the District Courts of the
United States, Southern District of New York"

usually sloops-of-war, gun brigs, or schooners. Most officers did not like convoy duty, which could be tedious and frequently meant arguments with commercial shipmasters. Furthermore, the region's extensive fogs often made it impossible to see the flags used in the Royal Navy's complex signalling system. The potential advantage for naval officers was that convoy duty presented an ideal opportunity to impress seamen.

With cruising, on the other hand, officers could use their own initiative to pursue and capture enemy shipping or privateers and receive prize money. In fighting the privateers, British naval officers quickly learned to disguise their vessels in order to lure US ships closer. Commander Henry Jane of H.M.S. *Indian* painted one side of his vessel black and dirtied the other side, rearranged the ship's boats, unsquared the yards,[3] and flew an American flag in order to look like a harmless merchant vessel. The ruse worked well enough to capture at least one US merchant brig.

In the summer of 1812, panic began to set in among Americans around the Bay of Fundy. At the beginning of August, the frigates *Maidstone* and *Spartan* briefly entered the bay and aggressively hunted down Yankee privateers, even launching raids on US harbours. The results were good, and a number of US privateers were captured (see Table 1). Yet there always seemed to be more of these irksome craft to replace their losses. Indeed, in the opening weeks of the war, despite the Royal Navy's efforts, New Brunswick's leadership was worried by the many US privateers operating in the bay. The region's newspapers complained that US privateers were "swarming around our coast, and in the Bay of Fundy; hardly a day passes but hear of captures made by them."

---

3   Royal Navy vessels were well known for being orderly and neat, including keeping
    their yards — the spars that supported the ship's sails — at a ninety-degree angle
    to the keel and perfectly perpendicular to the masts. By putting her yards askew or
    unsquaring them, *Indian*'s commander was attempting to make her look like a slov-
    enly merchant ship rather than the well-disciplined fighting ship she actually was.

SIGNALS to be made by the Ships of the Convoy as well as the Ships of War.

Yellow, Red, and Yellow	Foretopmast head	To signify that an enemy is in sight. Merchant ships not having this flag, are to signify the same by hoisting an English ensign at the maintopmast head with the union downwards
	Foretopmast head.	Land discovered.
	Foretopmast shrouds	To signify being overpressed with sail, and unable to keep company on that account.
	Maintopmast shrouds	Needing the assistance of boats to tow.
	Mizentopmast head, or Gaff end.	Being in distress, but not wanting immediate assistance
Ditto, with the union downwards	Foretopmast head.	Being in distress, and wanting immediate assistance.
	Foretopmast shrouds.	Being in distress, and obliged to part company on that account, when the state of the weather will not admit of acquainting the Commander of the convoy with the occasion thereof.
	Mizentopmast head, or Gaff end.	Being in danger, or sticking on a shoal. Fire guns until relieved.
A Wheft.	Foretopmast head.	To speak with the Commander of the convoy.
Union Jack.	Maintopmast head, or where best seen, except the Maintopmast shrouds.	To signify that the ships of the convoy see and understand the signal made to them by the Commander of the convoy.
	Maintopmast shrouds	To signify that the signal made by the Commander of the convoy is not distinct, or understood.

NAME	RIG	CANNON	CREW	CAPTOR	DATE	LOCATION	NOTES
Active	schooner	2	20	*Spartan*	July 16	off Cape Sable	
Fair Trader	schooner	1	20	*Indian & Plumper*	July 16	Bay of Fundy	
Argus	schooner	1	23	*Plumper*	July 17	Bay of Fundy	
Friendship	schooner	1	8	*Plumper*	July 18	Bay of Fundy	
Actress	sloop	4	53	*Spartan*	July 18	off Cape St. Mary	
Intention	schooner	1 & 3 swivels	29	*Spartan*	July 19	off Annapolis	
Gleaner	sloop	6	40	*Colibri*	July 23	off Cape Sable	
Curlew	brig	16	172	*Acasta*	July 24	off Cape Sable	270 tons & pierced for 20 guns; taken into service by Nova Scotia as a patrol vessel
Catherine	ship	14	88	*Colibri*	July 26	off Cape Sable	running fight for 1½ hours
Gossamer	brig	14	100	*Emulous*	July 30	off Cape Sable	some British prisoners on board
Morning Star	schooner	1 & 4 swivels	50	*Maidstone & Spartan*	August 1	Bailey's Mistake, ME	burned by boat party
Polly	schooner	1 & 4 swivels	40	*Maidstone & Spartan*	August 1	Bailey's Mistake, ME	burned by boat party
Commodore Barry	revenue cutter	6	75	*Maidstone & Spartan*	August 3	Little River, ME	brought out by the boats; most of the crew escaped

TABLE 1: AMERICAN PRIVATEERS CAPTURED IN OR NEAR THE BAY OF FUNDY, SUMMER 1812

NAME	RIG	CANNON	CREW	CAPTOR	DATE	LOCATION	NOTES
Madison	schooner	2	?	*Maidstone & Spartan*	August 3	Little River, ME	brought out by the boats; most of the crew escaped
Olive	schooner	2	?	*Maidstone & Spartan*	August 3	Little River, ME	brought out by the boats; most of the crew escaped
Spence	schooner	2	?	*Maidstone & Spartan*	August 3	Little River, ME	brought out by the boats; most of the crew escaped
Polly	schooner	4	35	*Colibri & Statira*	August 11	entrance to Bay of Fundy	
Buckskin	schooner	1 & 3 swivels	32	*Colibri & Statira*	August 11	off Cape Sable	
Dolphin	schooner	1 & 1 swivel	28	*Earl of Moira*	August 12	off Shelburne	*Earl Moira* was a Nova Scotia patrol vessel
Regulator	schooner	1	40	*Colibri*	August 12	off Cape Sable	
Dolphin	schooner	2	48	*Colibri & Maidstone*	August 13	off Cape Sable	
Lewis	schooner	6	30	*Hope*	August 14	off Halifax	*Hope*, tender to *África*
Pythagoras	schooner	3	35	*Bream*	August 19	off Shelburne	after an action of 20 minutes
Bunker Hill	schooner	7	72	*Belvedira*	August 21	Sambro Light-house, N.W. 242 miles	

Source: Based largely on the report of Vice-Admiral Herbert Sawyer to the Admiralty, August 25, 1812, reproduced in *London Gazette*, September 22, 1812.

US naval officer John Barry, namesake of the revenue cutter *Commodore Barry*. LC-H261 2945

Anxious to protect local commerce, Governor George Stracey Smyth and his council agreed that New Brunswick should acquire an armed vessel to protect shipping in the bay. On July 5, 1812 — just one week after news of war reached the colony — the Executive Council authorized the purchase of a vessel to defend New Brunswick against US privateers. A suitable craft was soon found in the *Commodore Barry*, a captured US revenue cutter that had been pierced for ten guns but that was carrying just six when taken. The schooner was named after John Barry, an Irish-born naval officer who served in the Continental Navy during the American Revolution and was the first officer commissioned in the US Navy when it was created in 1794. The US government purchased the schooner at Sag Harbor, New York, for $4,100 and stationed it at Passamaquoddy, Maine, under the command of Daniel Elliott, an experienced seaman who moved vigorously to suppress smuggling across the Maine-New Brunswick border.

The war was only a few weeks old when Elliott and his command, along with the American privateer *Madison*, found themselves bottled up in Little River, a narrow cove in eastern Maine. Outside lay four British warships, including the two frigates dispatched to the Bay of Fundy to sweep up the troublesome Yankee privateers that were interfering with local shipping. Battle was not long in coming, and it was to combine the elements of land and shore combat so common to littoral warfare. The *Commodore Barry*, in company with the small privateers *Madison*, *Olive*, and *Spruce* had no escape route. The Yankees therefore hauled their vessels close to shore and hastily built a "battery of cord wood" from which to defend the vessels. This "battery" was probably no more than a pile of firewood hastily rearranged to shelter US sailors as they fired their muskets. The British attacked on August 3 in five barges containing about two hundred and fifty sailors and Royal Marines from H.M.S. *Indian, Plumper, Spartan*, and *Maidstone*. It was the standard sort of skirmish the Royal Navy had become quite good at, often referred to "cutting out expeditions" or "boat parties." Such cutting out attacks were among the hardest-fought engagements of the War of 1812, but younger officers were keen on them because they offered relief from the tedium of patrol, blockade, and convoy, the opportunity to acquire prize money from captured vessels, and a chance to be noticed by their superiors and perhaps gain promotion.

One such midshipman was twenty-year-old Frederick Marryat of H.M.S. *Spartan*, who commanded a boat that helped to cut out the *Commodore Barry*. After the war, Marryat became one of the earliest novelists to work within the sea story genre, and wrote a number of best sellers, including *Mr. Midshipman Easy*, published in 1836. He essentially created the format that followed a midshipman through his sailing career, making him the precursor to twentieth-century novelists such as C.S. Forester, Patrick O'Brian, and their imitators. Marryat, however, was not the only aspiring author on board H.M.S. *Spartan*: her commander, Captain Edward Pelham Brenton, wrote a popular mammoth multi-volume *Naval History of Great Britain from the Year 1783 to 1822*, published in 1823.

Accounts of the skirmish are conflicting and fragmentary. The local community heard heavy gunfire for about two hours before the British overwhelmed the Americans, who had probably run short of ammunition. US newspapers claimed that, after a "severe contest, in which a number of the English were said to be killed," the crews of both the cutter and the privateer escaped because they "took to the woods" to avoid capture. Three of the *Commodore Barry*'s crew, however, were taken when Captain Brenton sent a detachment of ten Royal Marines to secure the revenue cutter. The British then burned the privateer *Madison* and took the *Commodore Barry* and the other two privateers to Saint John. On Thursday, August 6, *Spartan* and *Maidstone* arrived in Saint John harbour with seven prizes, including the two privateers and the revenue cutter. The American prisoners of war were landed and imprisoned in the city's jail. One can imagine that the city's populace was well pleased with the captures.

The Provincial Sloop *Brunswicker*
When the captured *Commodore Barry* entered Saint John harbour, merchants William Pagan, Hugh Johnstone, and Nehemiah Merritt

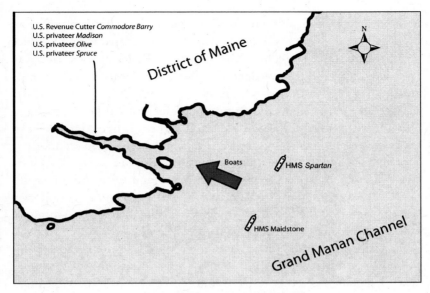

Cutting out the *Commodore Barry*
in Little River, Maine, August 1812. Joshua M. Smith

immediately recognized that the vessel was well-suited for the colony's needs. Not much is known about her appearance, let alone why she attracted the merchants' attention. She was not a large vessel — certainly less than one hundred tons displacement. When in US service, she apparently had been rigged first as a schooner, but records in New Brunswick and elsewhere always refer to her as a sloop.[4] It seems likely she was re-rigged as a single-masted vessel at some point before her capture, a fairly common transition in the age of sail. Her small size was probably attractive to her economy-minded purchasers because she would require a smaller crew. She was fully equipped and armed, although the details of her armament remain unknown. She also likely was built a little more substantially than the captured privateers then in

---

4   Schooners in this period usually had two masts; sloops had only one. The
     Commodore Barry entered US government service as a two-masted schooner, but
     apparently before its capture had been was re-rigged as a sloop, a fairly common
     transition in a time when captains frequently changed the rig.

harbour, which probably were no more than converted fishing schooners. As a matter of practicality, the vessel was also immediately available.

But there was a problem: while the United States had declared war on Britain, formal British recognition of the state of war did not yet exist, and so Nova Scotia's Vice-Admiralty Court, which handled all prize cases, could not formally condemn the vessel and sell her. Such legal formalities would not be allowed to stand in the way of colonial defence needs, however, so on August 8 the three merchants created an informal agreement whereby the Royal Navy officers would receive £1,250, in return for which the officers promised that their agent would steer the paperwork through the Vice-Admiralty Court and hand the sloop over "for the service of the Province." Included in the price were all its guns, ammunition, stores, provisions, boats, and everything else on board.

Initially, Governor Smyth refused to purchase the sloop for the colony, but within days, as his anxiety about American privateers increased, he purchased the "revenue cutter prize sloop" for the same price Pagan, Johnstone, and Merritt had paid for her. She was soon renamed *Brunswicker* to reflect her intended role in defending the colony's shipping. On August 20, the colonial government advertised in the Saint John newspapers for a contractor willing to supply provisions for its new sloop.

The sloop was quickly put in operational order and remained busy for the rest of 1812. Her mission was always defensive: to protect local shipping in the Bay of Fundy primarily by acting as an escort vessel. In mid-August, the colony provided instructions and a strict admonition that on no occasion was *Brunswicker* to go west of Passamaquoddy Bay unless in actual pursuit of an enemy vessel. Despite these instructions, *Brunswicker* made one cruise as far west as Mount Desert Island in the company of H.M. brig *Plumper* to rescue British-flagged vessels that had been captured by US privateers. Then, in September, the governor and council received a letter from *Plumper*'s commander urging that *Brunswicker* be released to cruise as far west as Mount Desert:

> From undoubted information which I have received, and
> from recent orders which have fallen into my hands from

the late captures I have made, I learn that the enemy's cruisers in general direct their prizes to make Mount Desert, where I had the good fortune to re-capture the three British vessels I brought into port, and had I the smallest assistance to take care of these I had in possession, I might have taken seven more; but the small privateers are so numerous that I could not quit my prizes. I was therefore under the painful necessity of allowing the enemy to pass unnoticed. There are at present from fifteen to twenty privateers out of Portland, Salem, and Boston, cruising on the Eastern coast of Nova Scotia, most of whom will be returning the latter end of this month; until then the coast will remain clear for their prizes to get in, as I can hear of no British cruisers in the Bay. I have therefore to request that His Honor the President would allow the *Brunswicker* to accompany His Majesty's brig under my command for a few days to Mount Desert, when, I have no doubt, we should intercept many British vessels getting into the enemy's ports before the Admiral has time to send a sufficient force there, of which I shall apprise him of the necessity without loss of time.

The council immediately recommended the employment of thirty or more additional hands, not exceeding fifty in the whole, on board *Brunswicker* to accompany *Plumper* on this service. A month later, the sloop again joined *Plumper* in escorting a convoy of fourteen merchant ships from Saint John to Halifax. In November, *Brunswicker* accompanied H.M. schooner *Bream* in quest of two US privateers said to be off Point Lepreau, chasing them off but failing to capture them. More than twenty seamen belonging to different ships in Saint John harbour and several local citizens volunteered their services on board *Brunswicker* for this duty.

Council member Beverly Robinson, who called
Brunswicker "paultry." NBM W6726

In December, *Brunswicker*, again in company with *Bream*, had the grim task of salvaging the wreck of *Plumper*, which, on the morning of December 5, had been caught in a snowstorm in the Bay of Fundy as it made its way from Halifax to Saint John and wrecked on rocks near Dipper Harbour, in Charlotte County. About half the people on board, including two female passengers, died. Two officers, including its commander, and twenty eight of the crew survived the ordeal and got ashore; some were taken aboard *Brunswicker* and transported to Saint John a few days later. On board *Plumper* was some $60,000 in silver Spanish dollars, the pay for New Brunswick's military garrison, so *Brunswicker* remained near the wreck for some weeks to guard it while salvors rescued $32,440 from the deep.

Despite this activity, the early months of 1813 saw the colonial government debating the value of the sloop. Governor Smyth told the council in January that he was convinced US forces would attack New Brunswick before spring. He regarded *Brunswicker* as a crucial element in the colony's defence and asked the council to authorize £500 to fund her operations for four months. The council agreed, but somewhat reluctantly. Beverly Robinson, in particular, worried about the utility of the vessel, which he called "paultry." Others thought that the vessel could aid in the defence of St. Andrews, although Robinson observed that the vessel's two 9-pounder cannon and 12-pound carronades provided little real firepower. Chief Justice Jonathan Bliss took a lighter view, jesting that, if *Brunswicker* went to St. Andrews, perhaps she should be insured so the colony could turn a profit if she were captured. Despite the jokes about insurance, *Brunswicker* visited St. Andrews by the end of January before returning to Saint John, and returned to Passamaquoddy Bay in early March.

Brunswicker's Officers and Crew

Brunswicker's commander for most of its career in provincial service was a mariner named James Reed, born in Saint John in 1784 to English parents who had settled in New Brunswick before the Loyalist migration. Reed went to sea as a young man and eventually became a ship's master, sailing principally between Saint John and ports in Britain. He was active in Saint John's social life as a member of the Freemasons and participated as an officer in a special volunteer militia unit designated as "sea fencibles" — militia who could serve either ashore or afloat. His background was ideal for his duties as commander of the armed sloop.

Much less is known about the rest of the crew — sailors in the age of sail are a notoriously difficult group to track — but some details can be gleaned from a document in the New Brunswick Provincial Archives that lists the crew (see Table 2). The officers were mostly from Saint John, and it seems likely that they were Reed's friends or family — the second mate, in particular, was probably his son or a nephew. The gunner was not a seaman but a soldier from the Royal Artillery who received additional

"View of the Town of St. Andrew's with its magnificent Harbour and Bay," ca. 1840. Coloured lithograph by William Day (Day and Son Lithographers) after a sketch by Frederick Wells. LAC C-016386

pay to serve on board *Brunswicker* and train her crew in the use of the cannon. The cook, Samuel Bagley, was black, and Richard Smith might have been as well. Both were illiterate, signing with a mark rather than a signature, as did seamen Robert Filler and Andrew Roark. The regular crew sometimes was joined by volunteers known as "supernumeraries," who rounded out the ship's complement when Reed anticipated combat. These were probably young local men who signed up for perhaps a week on a lark, serving for free except for provisions and the possibility of prize money. A week's service on board a tiny vessel in the dead of winter was probably more than enough for most volunteers, who undoubtedly were glad to return to hearth and home after their little adventure.

Although the sloop's officers and crew were not in the military or naval service, they did operate under strict ship's articles — a sort of contract that bound seamen to the master of a vessel. A copy of *Brunswicker*'s articles in the Provincial Archives of New Brunswick details the obligation of the crew to follow orders, not go ashore on pain of forfeiting their wages, and abide by the officers' rule for the "suppression of vice and immorality."

The bills generated by *Brunswicker*, also preserved in the Provincial Archives, offer some clues about life on board the vessel, especially diet. The food seems to have consisted entirely of fresh beef and ship's biscuit, or hardtack. Other grocery items included coffee, sugar, water, and, of course, rum. This basic diet was considerably less varied than that of the Royal Navy, which also provided peas, cheese, and cocoa on a regular basis. But no mention is made of any sort of vegetable, not even potatoes, on board *Brunswicker*. It is possible that, since the vessel spent much of the time in port, her crew was able to supplement their diet while ashore, and almost certainly they tried their luck with hook and line to catch fish.

Brunswicker's bills also indicate that the vessel needed repairs in early 1813. On the advice of some maritime gentlemen, including a Lieutenant Hare of the Royal Navy (of whom we shall hear more in the next chapter), colonial officials agreed to "fill in the waist" of the sloop, which probably involved replacing an open railing, and within a few weeks Saint John shipwrights had built a solid cedar bulwark on board. The choice of cedar is surprising, since, when hit by a cannonball, it was

TABLE 2: OFFICERS AND CREW OF *BRUNSWICKER*, JANUARY-FEBRUARY 1813		
NAME	**RANK**	**WAGES**
James Reed	commander	£10
Robert Pattison	chief mate	£7
James Reed	second mate	£5
William McDonald	carpenter	£5
Thomas Scott	gunner	£1 10s
John Noonan	seaman	£4
Samuel Berry	seaman	£4
William Britt	seaman	£4
Robert Filler	seaman	£4
Samuel Jones	seaman	£4
Robert McCurdy	seaman	£4
Barnard Lacky	seaman	£4
William Whitten	seaman	£4
Charles Scott	seaman	£4
Samuel Bagley	cook	£4
Richard Smith	seaman	£4
James McVeal	seaman	£4
Alexander McVeal	seaman	£4
Andrew Roark	seaman	£4
Mr. Rice	supernumerary	
William McBride	supernumerary	
John Smyley	supernumerary	
Daniel Bandon	supernumerary	
George Fairplay	supernumerary	
Samuel Brown	supernumerary	
William Hicks	supernumerary	
James Hutchinson	supernumerary	

Source: Provincial Archives of New Brunswick, Sessional Records (RS24) S23-R10.13.

Governor George Stracey Smyth. LAC C-011221

notoriously prone to splintering, sending a shower of shrapnel-like shards that could maim or kill those nearby.

Bills, however, were *Brunswicker*'s undoing. The expense of running the vessel was prohibitive: from August 1812 until January 2, 1813, it exceeded £771, a serious drain on the colony's finances. When, on January 21, Governor Smyth announced that the Crown would bear the cost no longer, the colonial legislature balked at assuming the responsibility and resolved that the sloop should be discharged from service since there was now a sufficient Royal Navy presence to protect local shipping. Smyth, who had been heavily censured by the Colonial Office in London for having taken the vessel into service, was in no position to disagree. According to the Vice-Admiralty Court records now in Ottawa, *Brunswicker* was laid up in May 1813 and remained in Saint John harbour for a further two years under the care of a shipkeeper, stripped of its sails and much of its rigging. Mostly, she sat at a mooring, where she was pumped out occasionally and had her sails aired.

Ironically, *Brunswicker* was deactivated just as panic over US privateers swept Saint John. In early May, word arrived that an American privateer was skulking outside the harbour, but there were no British naval vessels in the vicinity. Rather than reactivate *Brunswicker*, Saint John merchants took over the Salem privateer *Cossack*, which had been launched just that spring and captured between Grand Manan Island and West Quoddy Light on its first cruise by H.M. sloop *Emulous* and taken to Saint John for adjudication. A schooner of only forty-eight tons, she boasted but one cannon, a long 18-pounder. After her capture, she sat at a wharf in Saint John with her sails stripped from her and placed in a warehouse. Alarmed by rumours of nearby privateers, local merchants prevailed on officials to release the vessel to guard the harbour. Sailors re-rigged the privateer's sails, and arrangements were made for soldiers of the Saint John garrison to embark on the schooner as marines. James Reid offered to command the vessel, an entirely logical choice given his experience. The US threat soon passed, however, and the vessel remained anchored in the harbour. On his return to Saint John, the commander of *Emulous* was displeased to see "his" prize vessel ready to get under way and took the schooner to Halifax without notifying anyone, sparking a court case in Nova Scotia's Vice-Admiralty Court.

For the remainder of the war, the business of defending New Brunswick's trade and coasts fell once again on the heavily burdened shoulders of the Royal Navy. The colony was extraordinarily lucky that the young officer most associated with that duty not only was unusually willing but also able to carry out that mission.

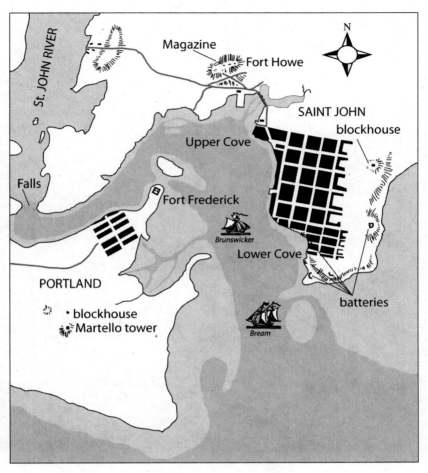

Saint John, circa late 1812. Its fortifications, however, were in poor repair or, in the case of the Martello Tower, not yet constructed.

Joshua M. Smith, based on W.O. 55/860, p. 422

Bream in combat with the American privateer *Pythagoras*, 1812. MM

Chapter Three

Bream Brings the War to the Enemy

Military theorist Karl von Clausewitz defined "friction" in part as making the simplest things difficult, and he often referred to it as the "fog of war." This is a singularly appropriate term for the Bay of Fundy, where fogs can cling to the shoreline for weeks at a time. In his influential book, *On War*, Clausewitz wrote, "The great uncertainty of all data in war is a peculiar difficulty, because all action must, to a certain extent, be planned in a mere twilight, which in addition not infrequently — like the effect of a fog or moonshine — gives to things exaggerated dimensions and unnatural appearance."

The British *guerre de course* in the Bay of Fundy and adjacent waters achieved great success because the American foe, befuddled by the fog of war, could not perceive how minuscule was the force opposing it. Colonial privateers and British warships took advantage of the friction in spring 1813, taking the war to the enemy by capturing or destroying US shipping travelling along the Maine coast, threatening military supply lines. In one instance, the sloop-of-war *Rattler* captured an American supply schooner loaded with government stores for the troops at Eastport off West Quoddy Light, only a few miles from its destination. Feeding its troops should have been easy for the United States, but the fog of war left many coastal outposts in Maine on short rations.

The war in the Gulf of Maine region might have been petty, but it still had some important patterns that are informative about the nature of littoral warfare. In particular, the war fought by the tiny British naval schooner *Bream* (pronounced "Brim" like the species of fish) reveals how small units fought this war. *Bream* was not a glamorous vessel by any means. Just fifty-five feet long and about seventy-two tons burthen, her one claim to fame was that she had delivered the sailors impressed from the U.S.S. *Chesapeake* in 1807 back to the United States in 1812 — five years after the *Chesapeake* incident and a full month after war broke out between the United States and Britain. Otherwise, *Bream* was an ordinary, hardworking naval vessel, employed in numerous duties during the War of 1812, mostly in the waters off New England and the Maritime colonies; although, by the end of 1814, she had shifted operations to Chesapeake Bay.

Bream belonged to an unfortunate class of schooners built in Bermuda that had the unhappy distinction of being named after fish. In his *Naval History of Great Britain*, William James repeatedly derides them, referring to them as "cock-boats" and "tom-tit cruisers." "These vessels," says James, "were a disgrace to the British navy. They were built at Bermuda, of the pencil-cedar, measured about 78 tons, mounted four 12-pounder carronades, and were manned with 20 men and boys. In point of force, three of them united were not more than a match for a single gunboat, as usually armed. Their very appearance as 'men of war' raised a laugh at the expense of the projector. Many officers refused to take the command of them." He also notes that the "bulwark, if it deserved the name, [of these ships] consisted, with here and there a small timber, of an outside and an inside plank." Of thirty schooners in this class, twenty-seven were captured or foundered; only three, including *Bream*, survived to be sold out of the service. James concludes that "these 'king's schooners' were found to sail wretchedly, and proved so crank and unseaworthy that almost every one of them that escaped capture went to the bottom with the unfortunate men on board." Other authorities disparaged cedar as a shipbuilding material for warships, claiming that cedar splintered far worse than the more traditional oak or fir when hit by cannon fire, creating a shower of splinters that lacerated crew members.

Royal Navy 12-pounder carronade on a truck carriage, common weapons on small vessels such as *Bream*.

Cooke, *Ships & Ways of Other Days*

James's comments are in a sense fortuitous, for little is known about the Royal Navy's smaller vessels during the War of 1812, and without his acerbic comments these ships might have slipped entirely into oblivion. Few writers have tried to assess their utility, contribution to British naval efforts, especially in North American waters, or James's dismissal of them as "a disgrace to the British navy."

The armament and crew were scanty as well: the official armament of this class of vessels consisted of four 12-pounder carronades and they carried a crew of twenty, although *Bream* seems to have carried two additional 6-pounder cannon and a crew of forty during the war. *Bream* was a gaff-rigged, two-masted topsail schooner,[1] and, as one of its commanders commented, her "sailing qualities were of the most inferior order." Her small size and fore-and-aft rig allowed the vessel to blend in with US coastal shipping (especially with the topmasts sent down[2]), a potential benefit in fighting a war, but it was offset by cramped quarters, a deck constantly awash in winter weather, and limited space for provisions. In terms of size, rig, and armament, *Bream* was remarkably similar to her

---

1   On gaff-rigged ships, the biggest sails were suspended from a yard or spar that was hoisted up by the crew. *Bream* had two masts with gaff-rigged sails.

2   Some ships — usually those, such as warships and privateers, that needed more speed — sometimes had smaller masts attached atop their main masts, with spars to support an additional set of small square sails. These "top masts" could be removed and sent down to the deck before a storm or if the captain wished to disguise the ship as a coasting schooner.

opponents, the small privateers from Salem that preyed on British and colonial shipping in the Bay of Fundy and the waters off Nova Scotia.

Operations in 1813

In spring 1813, British warships and colonial privateers went on the offensive, ravaging US maritime trade in the Gulf of Maine. There were no American naval ships in the region — in March the US Navy had withdrawn its sole active gunboat that operated out of Portland. Newspaper editors in Maine bemoaned the depredations of the British navy and asked why the US Navy did nothing to protect coastal commerce. Tiny *Bream* played her part in riling the newspapermen, capturing dozens of small fishing boats and coasting craft — some as small as canoes. *Bream*'s diminutive size often deceived US ships, which assumed she was just a fishing vessel. An American newspaper described *Bream* and her activities as she lay at anchor off the coast:

> A gentleman who arrived in town last evening, informs us he was on Monhegan-island April 18th, and saw from hence that day, a British armed [schooner] of 8 guns, lying close under the island, with her sails down, and main topmast launched. In the morning her armed barge captured a coasting sloop, which after passing and repassing of boats, was dismantled, scuttled and sunk. Saw the same [schooner] soon after, on the same day, capture and burn two coasting [schooners] and [chase] two others, but which made their escape. As he came out the next morning, saw the same armed vessel close into the island, with her sails down as before, having in co. a sloop, supposed to have been captured during the night. — She was afterwards seen to bring to a sloop to windward.

The prizes *Bream* captured reveal coastal trade patterns, whereby high-bulk, low-value cargoes, such as timber or plaster or cordwood, were carried westward to commercial centres such as Boston, while foodstuffs and West India goods, such as rum and molasses, headed east. As Table 3 and the accompanying map reveal, the waters between Monhegan and Seguin islands and Boothbay were a chokepoint that even a tiny patrol vessel such as *Bream* could throttle. The value of many of these cargoes and vessels often was nominal, especially of those in ballast, but for the fragile communities of downeast Maine, these craft carried life's essentials, especially provisions such as flour and corn that would get them through the spring "starving time." *Bream* might have been small, but she squeezed the already precarious food supply of thousands of Mainers, who were not self-sufficient in food and had to import many provisions. A letter writer in Buckstown, on the Penobscot River, complained that, in late April, a British vessel, almost certainly *Bream*, "burnt a sloop belonging to this town — previous to burning her they threw overboard several bags of corn, her anchors, &c." The unknown correspondent concluded, "The scarcity of grain, and provisions generally, is very great. Starvation is commencing. It is stated that a woman and two children starved during the winter in one of the back settlements." Similar statements were common in other New England newspapers.

Tables and maps, however, cannot tell the full story — Table 3 reveals only those prizes that made it to the Maritime colonies and successfully underwent the arduous prize adjudication system of the Vice-Admiralty Courts. For example, *Bream* captured the schooner *Cranberry*, which was empty, at the same time as the dilapidated old schooner *Dolphin*, with a cargo of provisions. *Bream*'s crew then placed the *Dolphin*'s cargo on board the *Cranberry* and released the older vessel. This seems to have been a common practice; a Saint John newspaper reported that, of six vessels *Bream* captured in late April, five were burnt "after stripping them of their most valuable materials." A prisoner on board *Bream* reported his melancholy on seeing so many vessels in flames.

Like many small vessels, *Bream* was incapable of sustained operations on her own: she was a "short-legged" vessel that operated best when she had access to a hospital, fresh beef, and vegetables. Thus, operating on short cruises out of Saint John was ideal for this craft. A close analysis of her logbook reveals how *Bream* operated in 1813. She was under way for

	DATE	PRIZE NAME	RIG	TONNAGE	LOCATION	CARGO
❶	March 27*	*Cranberry*	schooner		Bass Harbor	provisions
❷	March 27*	*Two Brothers*	schooner	131	Bass Harbor	cordwood
❸	March 31	*Neptune*	schooner	98	off Boothbay	timber, cordwood
❹	March 31	*Defiance*	schooner	113	off Boothbay	cordwood
❺	April 12*	*Alexander*	ship	308	Kennebunk Beach	privateer
❻	April 19	*Lark*	sloop	70	off Boothbay	mixed
❼	April 20	*Susannah*	sloop	89	off Monhegan	cordwood
❽	April 23	*Semerimes*	sloop	85	off Monhegan Island	timber, cordwood
❾	April 26	*Branch*	schooner	78	off Monhegan Island	ballast
❿	April 27	*Pilgrim*	boat	25	West Quoddy	mixed
⓫	May 13	*Sally*	schooner	74	off Little River	plaister, salt
⓬	July 12	*Jefferson*	schooner	99	Georges Island	ballast
⓭	July 14	*Betsy*	schooner	117	west of Seguin Island	rum
⓮	July 14	*Triton*	schooner	122	west of Seguin Island	rum

TABLE 3: PRIZES CAPTURED BY *BREAM* IN MAINE WATERS, MARCH–JULY 1813.

* Taken in conjunction with H.M. sloop *Rattler*.
Source: Author's compilation from the newspaper *Eastern Argus* (Portland, ME).

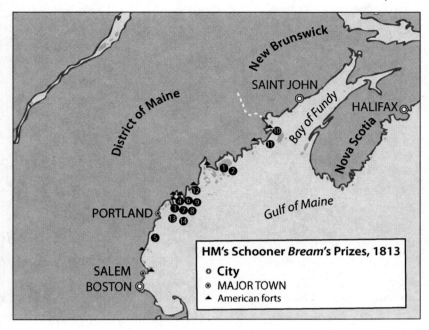

Location of prizes captured by *Bream* in Maine waters, March-July 1813.

Joshua M. Smith

approximately 157 days, at anchor for 189, and undergoing substantial repairs for about nineteen. She was under way longer than at anchor only during the peak shipping months of April through July and again in October; August and September were very foggy, which is typical of the Bay of Fundy in late summer, so that the vessel had to remain at anchor or proceed with shortened sail and frequent soundings.

Much of *Bream*'s time under way was spent cruising, actively patrolling the Bay of Fundy and the Maine coast in search of American privateers. The number of days she was under way correlates to the number of prizes she took: out of ten prizes successfully prosecuted in the Vice-Admiralty Courts, *Bream* captured eight between April and July — five in April alone, the month *Bream* was under way most. More significantly, *Bream* spent the most time in enemy waters in April, closely

Rattler, which saw much service in the Bay of Fundy region. Originally ship rigged, here she is rigged as a brig and was never the single-masted vessel that the term sloop might imply. Snider, *Under the Red Jack*

patrolling the Maine coast as far west as the Kennebunk River. Notably, *Bream* never ventured further west than Seguin Island unless accompanied by the sloop-of-war *Rattler*. Besides cruising, *Bream* sometimes spent her time under way transporting soldiers to outposts such as St. Andrews or convoying cargo vessels.

Things did not always go well for *Bream* when she pushed too far west, however, even when in the company of *Rattler*. In particular, going so far made it much more difficult to bring prize vessels back to port. In March 1813, for example, American soldiers stationed at Boothbay in mid-coast Maine manned three fishing boats and recaptured a schooner *Bream* had taken, along with her prize crew of two sailors. The British prisoners revealed that their schooner would anchor in Boothbay harbour that night, joined by the much larger and more powerful *Rattler*. Forewarned, the Yankees prepared for a raid and called for reinforcements. When a landing party from *Rattler* came ashore, the Americans easily repulsed it in a bloodless skirmish.

Bream saw combat several times. One of the harder-fought actions was in capturing the American privateer sloop *Wasp* near Brier Island in the Bay of Fundy in August 1813. Built in Salem, the *Wasp* carried two 6-pounders and twenty-five men. Upon her first cruise, after taking a few prizes, she encountered *Bream* and ran. For nine hours, the Salem captain tried every trick he knew to shake the Royal Navy schooner, which remained within musket range almost the entire time. Finally, *Bream* closed with the privateer and a fierce half-hour battle ensued that resulted in the *Wasp*'s surrender. Brought to Saint John, the American commander and his crew were treated with surprising kindness. On parole and thus free to walk the streets, the Yankee commander was pointed out by Saint John residents as the Salem captain who had defended his vessel with heroism.

The one tactic most likely to outfox *Bream* was for the intended prey to beach herself and for the crew to fight from shore. This would force the British vessel to send her boats after the quarry, almost completely negating the advantage the schooner's cannon might bestow. Two logbooks now preserved at the Maine Historical Society illustrate this point. For example, in December 1812, to evade *Bream*, the crew of the tiny American privateer *Lilly* ran their ship onshore and took shelter, "and then we histed English collers under American collars and took the trumpet and told them to come in and take them downe we was so near we could hear them talk." In October 1813, *Bream* pursued the privateer *Holker*, which, according to her logbook, ran into "Starbord Crik we then got on all our arms on shore & prepared to give them a warm reception but she bore away & went to their old anchorage." Discretion being the better part of valour, these boat parties carefully appraised the situation before coming within gunshot. If militia collected to defend a beached vessel, the boat parties usually called off their attack.

In the last week of April 1813, incensed by *Bream*'s destruction of

US shipping, Maine residents gathered under the leadership of Captain Samuel Tucker to capture the British schooner. Tucker, a veteran of the Continental Navy, was no longer a young man but was well qualified to lead such an expedition. The coasting schooner *Increase* was outfitted with a crew of forty-seven, each of whom agreed to bring his own musket, ammunition, and provisions for a week-long cruise. Tucker used his reputation and political clout to procure a privateering commission that allowed the *Increase* legally to seize enemy ships. He also borrowed some small cannon and ammunition from the US Army garrison at Fort Edgecomb, near Wiscasset. Tucker and his men patrolled the Maine coast for two days seeking the elusive *Bream*, but failed to find her.

Anxious to resume their spring ploughing, the crew returned the borrowed cannon and sailed home. On rounding Pemaquid Point, they spied a suspicious vessel. In a sharp battle, Tucker and his men overwhelmed the enemy ship with small-arms fire and then boarded her. After the battle, the commander of the British ship marvelled that "there is above 300 balls in our hull and spars, the sails and rigging of both vessels wonderfully cut to pieces, a number of balls through our hats and cloaths, yet there is not a man either killed or wounded on either side." The Americans discovered, however, that their captured vessel was not *Bream*, but the tiny privateer *Crown* out of Halifax. Captain Tucker landed the prisoners and marched them to Wiscasset, where he handed them over to federal authorities.

The defeat and capture of *Crown* must have provided at least a moment of relief for the citizens and soldiers of the area, even if it was not the bothersome *Bream*. The local US deputy marshal granted Crown's Captain Jennings parole to wander the streets of Wiscasset if he pledged, on his honour, to not attempt to escape; his officers and men were confined in the Wiscasset jail before being transferred to the blockhouse at Fort Edgecomb. Jennings absconded, however, after sixty-four days in captivity; local tradition has it that he escaped dressed as a woman. After a brush with US soldiers in Eastport, he slipped across the border into New Brunswick and safety.

Lieutenant Charles Hare, R.N.

Bream was always commanded by a lieutenant, assisted by a master's mate and one or two midshipmen. The lieutenants seem to have been officers with little prospect of promotion; of *Bream*'s wartime commanders, none is known to have risen above lieutenant. *Bream*'s most important commander was Lieutenant Charles Hare, based out of Saint John.

Hare's life reads much like something from a Patrick O'Brian novel. Born in 1789 and named after his father, Charles spent his early childhood at Summer Castle, an estate belonging to his mother's relatives at the village of Fillingham, in Lincolnshire, England. His father was a naval officer and veteran of the American Revolutionary War whose active duty meant he missed most of Charles's early childhood. While in command of H.M. fireship *Vulcan* in late 1793, the elder Charles was wounded grievously. The British were evacuating Toulon, France, and

Lieutenant Charles Hare, R.N.
Courtesy of Hare Family

Summer Castle in Lincolnshire, where Charles Hare
spent his early childhood. Courtesy of Hare Family

decided to destroy the French fleet moored there rather than see it fall
into the hands of the revolutionaries. The method they chose was to ex-
plode *Vulcan* in the midst of the French ships, setting them on fire. Hare
sailed his vessel toward his target, then ordered the crew off, remaining
alone on board. As he prepared to depart the vessel, he fired his pistol
into the train leading to the magazine. The resultant explosion blew
him into the water "a vast distance" but happily near one of *Vulcan*'s
boats, and his shattered body was pulled from the water. He remained on
board H.M.S. *Victory* for nine months, initially blind and senseless. His
action destroyed thirteen French warships, however, and for his heroism
the Admiralty granted him a pension of £200 per annum. For a time, he
worked ashore as a gamekeeper on an estate, and the few years before he
returned to active duty were probably when his children came to know
him.

In 1801, the elder Hare returned to active duty in command of H.M.S.
Madras, taking with him his eleven-year-old eldest son as a volunteer first

class. This was a common practice at the time; the naval establishment as a whole approved of bringing "the children of the service" on board its warships at a young age. As naval historian N.A.M. Rodger notes in *The Command of the Sea*, "Many boys kissed their mothers goodbye at ten or twelve, and returned as men if they returned at all."

Father and son continued on *Madras* during the Egyptian campaign until the old captain died in late 1801 from complications related to his wounds. His body was interred on Malta. The younger Hare's response to his father's death is unrecorded, but he remained in the navy, and two of his younger brothers served as officers in the fleet as well. In 1802, he was on board *Amphion* for a time, serving under Thomas Masterman Hardy. He then transferred to the frigate *Minerve*, commanded by Jahleel Brenton (elder brother of Edward Brenton, commander of *Spartan* when it captured the *Commodore Barry* in 1812). Tragedy struck when *Minerve* was stranded in a dense fog off Cherbourg, France. Captain Brenton and his crew fought for ten hours against French shore batteries and gunboats, but it proved impossible to save the ship and they surrendered. The captors marched the survivors to Verdun, a fortress city hundreds of miles inland.

Captain Brenton boarded his midshipmen with locals and arranged for them to continue their general education, navigation, and French. He even wrote to Mrs. Hare to assure her that her son was not faring too badly. Young Charles, like many of his fellow imprisoned midshipmen, had taken to horseracing, gambling, and meals with the young men of Verdun. Brenton seems to have persuaded him to give up these pastimes but not without a little teenage sulking on Hare's part. After that, Hare applied himself to his studies. In fact, he gave up the liberties and easy life of Verdun altogether for close confinement in the prison at Sarre Libre (modern Saarlouis) in Germany. In an account still in the possession of the Hare family, he explains why he chose confinement over parole. While at Verdun, he had sworn on his honour not to escape. When closely incarcerated at Sarre Libre, however, he could in good conscience attempt to escape, although he was likely to be killed in the attempt or executed if caught. As his imprisonment in the fortress town

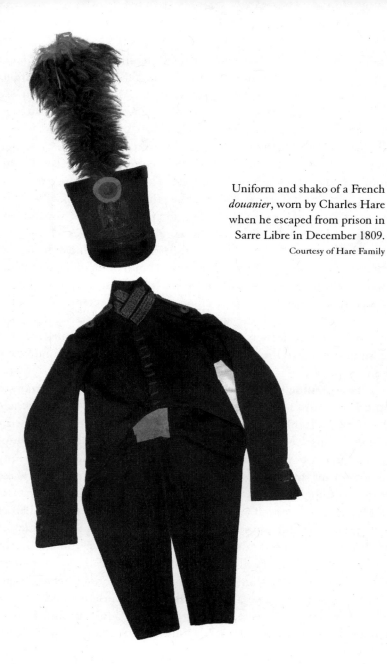

Uniform and shako of a French
douanier, worn by Charles Hare
when he escaped from prison in
Sarre Libre in December 1809.

Courtesy of Hare Family

gradually became less severe, he made friends in town and formulated an escape plan.

Hare made his bid for freedom in December 1809 dressed in the uniform of a customs officer, or *douanier*, which a sympathetic local had given him. He travelled some five hundred miles in seven days, accompanied by his dog and a guide. The French language skills he had picked up in prison paid off handsomely, but even he admitted that his escape was miraculous. Especially hair raising were encounters with other *douaniers* and French police, but he kept his cool and made it to the Netherlands, where sympathetic locals helped him find a boat that returned him to a British warship. A few days later, he was at his mother's home in England.

Hare quickly returned to duty, and on January 3, 1810, he passed his lieutenant's exam, receiving his commission on June 8, 1810. This is a little surprising, because while Hare met the age qualification, which was twenty, he did not seem to have the requisite six years' worth of sea time given the length of his imprisonment. It is possible the Admiralty or an unknown sponsor did him a favour by allowing him to sit for the gruelling exam. According to William O'Byrne's *Naval Biographical Dictionary*, Lieutenant Hare served briefly on a number of ships and was at the siege of Cadiz in Spain. In 1811, he served off South America on board *Porcupine*, then on board *Barbados* in the English Channel and the Caribbean. By late 1812, he was in New Brunswick, assigned to command the schooner *Bream*.

Hare proved an active officer who used his tiny command to bring the war to the enemy and protect British shipping. Saint John's merchants so approved of Hare and *Bream* that, in November 1813, they petitioned the Royal Navy to keep the vessel in the Bay of Fundy. Hare, however, captured a prize more valuable than any galleon: Mary Stewart McGeorge, the stepdaughter of John Black, Saint John's wealthiest merchant. A staunch Loyalist, Black was notable in Saint John for having illuminated his house to celebrate the British naval victories of the Nile and Trafalgar. It is not known how Hare met his future wife, but William Black, John's younger brother and a wealthy and powerful man in his own right, was *Bream*'s prize agent. On August 11, 1813, Hare married eighteen-year-old Mary in an Anglican ceremony. The next day, *Bream* set sail escorting a convoy, but not before firing a twenty-one-gun salute, ostensibly to celebrate the Prince Regent's birthday, but perhaps also as a *feu de joie* for the married couple. Young and successful, and now well connected with local society, Hare must have felt that the world was his oyster.

Hare had reason to feel good about himself: pouring in to augment his meagre lieutenant's pay was prize money from capturing US ships, bringing them into port (mostly Saint John), and having them condemned by the Vice-Admiralty Court in Halifax. Waiting for the court to adjudicate the prize, sell it, and hand the appropriate proceeds over to Hare and his crew could take many months, however, so a quicker, if less legitimate, method was to capture US vessels and return them to their owners in return for a ransom. For example, in December 1812, *Bream* captured the US coasting schooner *Ospray*, and by June 8, 1813, its master had agreed to pay his captors a little over two hundred and sixty dollars for his vessel's release. Evidently the schooner's master was a man of his word and he paid his ransom on time.

Hare could also be happy that his actions were getting some favourable attention from his superiors, including Sir John Borlase Warren, commander of the North American Station, who expressed his pleasure at Hare's exertions in the Bay of Fundy. By autumn 1813, some of his patrons were attempting to find a better vessel for him to command. Even Americans who encountered the commander of *Bream* expressed their admiration for him. One of Hare's Yankee prisoners called him "a fine man," recounting how he restored his prisoners' clothing without searching their trunks. A privateersman captured by the tiny schooner even published his thanks in newspapers on both sides of the border for the "very courteous, friendly and gentlemanlike treatment received while a prisoner on board, the deportment observed toward him being more like a friend and countryman than that of a declared enemy." Hare was not simply being a gentleman; he was being a smart commander. Leniency, even kindness, was not only in accord with the British government's decision to placate New Englanders; it also made Hare's job easier in the low-intensity style of warfare being fought in the Gulf of Maine and adjacent waters. Encouraging the enemy to fight more fiercely through ruthless behaviour would have severely undermined the effectiveness of a vessel as small as *Bream*. Not coincidentally, it also would have made it much more difficult to capture prizes and reap prize money. Hare, indeed, seemed to be a charismatic leader with the ability to inspire loyalty and even devotion among his crew, the respect of New Brunswickers, and the admiration of his prisoners. He was in almost every respect the ideal Royal Navy officer of the Regency period: a gentleman, fine sailor, and brave and cunning leader.

Bream's Crew

The personal lives of *Bream*'s crew remain obscure, but even without much detail they render surprises for the modern scholar. First among these is that, unlike most such tiny vessels, *Bream* carried a complement of Royal Marines, probably a corporal and four to six privates. Another surprise is that *Bream* often carried a number of "supernumeraries" — volunteers who joined the ship "for provisions and prize money." These volunteers were not gentlemen looking for a midshipman's berth, but local fishermen and mariners, valuable for their seafaring skills and local knowledge. Volunteers shipped either

Royal Marine, circa War of 1812.
New York Public Library 1199102

at Saint John or at the "Western Isles" in Passamaquoddy Bay, generally in summer, when sea conditions were gentle and the chances of prize money greatly improved.

Conditions aboard *Bream*, though, must have been grim at any time of year. Crowded, wet, leaky, and beset with rats that ate spare sails and even destroyed ammunition in the magazine, *Bream* was no pleasure craft. Lieutenant Hare departed from his characteristically terse logbook entries only once to reveal the dangers of operating such a small vessel in winter in the Bay of Fundy. On January 15, 1813, after fighting a storm for several days, he recorded, "The Gale increasing & the vessel pitching heavy, the spray of the Sea flew over her in all directions, it instantly froze, so that everything became a mere flake of Ice and a great many of the Crew with myself much frozen." Hare responded to the crisis in the typical naval fashion of the era: he issued an extra allowance of rum that day. When he returned to Saint John, several of his crew were put into the military hospital to recover from exposure and likely frostbite.

To maintain order on *Bream*, discipline had to be harsh. For example, on New Year's Day, 1813, while at anchor in Saint John harbour, the crew became drunk, and two men deserted. The next day, Hare flogged five of the crew, an eighth of its complement, for crimes related to their drunken spree. Hare had to borrow a boatswain's mate — the petty officer normally charged with maintaining order and meting out punishments — from H.M. brig *Nova Scotia* to flog the men because his own boatswain's mate, Donald McCloud, was one of the men being punished. McCloud and his four crewmates received a combined total of 128 lashes.

For many seamen, desertion was an attractive alternative to such harsh naval discipline, and *Bream* lost a substantial number of seamen this way. *Bream*'s logbook records that twelve sailors deserted the schooner in 1813. Their methods were various, but usually they slipped away while on leave or while serving in a shore party that was collecting firewood or water. Seaman David Wood, for example, was scooped up by the military in Saint John for "having been straggling," and Hare gave him a total of six dozen lashes, three dozen on September 3 and the remainder on September 7, even though naval regulations dictated that a captain could give a seaman no more than a dozen lashes at a time. Hare, like many of his contemporaries, ignored this regulation and meted out several dozen blows at a time. Most deserters never returned; indeed, as N.A.M. Rodger notes, smart officers sometimes actually encouraged desertion to get rid of useless or troublesome sailors. Perhaps Hare encouraged the deadwood among his crew to desert.

Replacements, however, had to be found for deserters. On occasion, a sailor would join voluntarily from a merchant ship, but pressed sailors far outnumbered volunteers. Over the course of 1813, *Bream* impressed a total of twelve seamen, nine of them in June, mainly from merchant vessels at anchor at Saint John. Some undoubtedly were Americans, and one seems to have escaped to tell his tale, but the official records do not substantiate his claim that no fewer than seventeen of *Bream*'s crew were Yankees.

Despite the often harsh conditions on board, *Bream*'s crew was surprisingly loyal to the ship, or perhaps to the charismatic Lieutenant Hare. In April 1813, an American privateer chased two of *Bream*'s crew ashore in Maine while manning a prize vessel; they walked over one hundred miles through enemy territory to rejoin the schooner at Passamaquoddy Bay. In November, another seaman walked all the way from Saint John to Halifax to rejoin *Bream*. The thought of prize money might have kept him warm on his trek; on Christmas Eve, Hare issued £80 to the crew, and that was only a portion of the money due them. But on December 19 a supernumerary deserted, suggesting that prize money alone was not enough to keep hands on board. Crew members also might have felt deep loyalty to shipmates or a sense of belonging to the Royal Navy that impelled at least some to remain with their ship despite the hardships they endured.

As a class, the four-gun schooners were not successful, but *Bream* appears to have been an exception. Under the able command of Charles Hare, this tiny vessel took war, confusion, and discomfort to the enemy, providing the "friction" about which Clausewitz wrote. Hare also developed ties to New Brunswick's commercial community, building enduring bonds between Britain and the Loyalist frontier colony through service and marriage.

Blood sculpsit.

Samuel Blyth Esqr.
Commander, RN.

Published 31st. Decr. 1814 by Joyce Gold, Naval Chronicle Office, 103, Shoe Lane, London.

Chapter Four

"The Sea-Fight Far Away":
H.M. Brig *Boxer* and the Fog of War

In 1813 the Royal Navy was able to dedicate more resources to the war in North American waters. The Halifax station began to receive more ships, and reinforcements were sent to the Bay of Fundy to protect shipping from the Americans. Among these reinforcements was a new vessel, H.M. brig *Boxer*. Launched in England in July 1812 and taken into the Royal Navy the next month, the brig fitted out at Portsmouth in the autumn of that year. In April 1813, *Boxer* was part of a convoy escort that crossed the Atlantic from Cork, Ireland, arriving in Halifax on May 20. By mid-June, she was convoying ships between Halifax and Saint John.

While considerably bigger than *Brunswicker* or *Bream*, *Boxer* was by no means large: not quite eighty-five feet long, with a beam of twenty-two feet. Jammed into this space was a crew of about seventy-five. Perhaps this is why such a brig-of-war was so heartily disliked by seamen. In one of Frederick Marryat's novels of the Napoleonic Wars, an experienced seaman proclaims that "they would certainly damn their inventor to all eternity" and that "their common, low names, *Pincher*, *Thrasher*, *Boxer*, *Badger*, and all that sort, are quite good enough for them." Another author says of this class of warship that they sailed like

Facing page: Commander Samuel Blyth. McHS OJ 359.09 N227 V32

colliers — slow-moving vessels that transported coal — and concludes they were likely to serve as the graves of both the lives and reputations of the officers and men who sailed them, an all-too-accurate depiction of *Boxer*'s brief naval career.

Boxer's only commander in her short career was Samuel Blyth. In 1809, Blyth had distinguished himself in an amphibious assault on Cayenne in French Guiana, an engagement that left him badly wounded. The British government recognized his valour by awarding him a sword. In 1811, as a lieutenant on board H.M.S. *Quebec*, he volunteered for a cutting-out expedition on the Dutch coast, during which he was wounded first in hand-to-hand combat and then by an explosion that blew him into the water. As N.A.M. Rodger points out in *The Command of the Ocean*, gallantry was the only avenue by which junior officers could seek promotion, and young, ambitious officers responded by behaving rashly in battle. Thus, Blyth's courage under fire earned him promotion to the rank of commander and he was given his own ship. He might well have seen his command of *Boxer* as a sort of apprenticeship, perhaps a stepping stone to the command of a sloop-of-war or frigate.

Blyth knew his job was to bring war to the enemy, and in summer 1813 *Boxer* became a scourge to US shipping, sending in nine prizes to Halifax, exclusive of vessels burnt or ransomed. An officer on board H.M.S. *Tenedos* noted that a possible reason for *Boxer*'s success was her innocuous appearance, writing "she was disguised like an American Bark, insomuch that 'twas impossible for any one to know her for a man of war, having her sides varnish'd, and altogether the appearance of a Yankee." At the end of June, *Boxer* was lurking near West Quoddy Lighthouse, and snapped up four prizes, which she sent into Saint John. A month later, she was cruising in Penobscot Bay, using her boats to enter small harbours and plunder vessels sheltered there.

Like *Bream*'s Lieutenant Charles Hare, Blyth exhibited the spirit of the age by being magnanimous toward the enemy. *Boxer* happened to be in Halifax harbour in summer 1813 when the frigate H.M.S. *Shannon* towed the captured frigate U.S.S. *Chesapeake* into the anchorage. In a brief, one-on-one battle, *Shannon* had pummelled the American ship and forced it to surrender. Blyth undoubtedly shared in the celebrations, but he also served as a pallbearer for James Lawrence, the captain of the *Chesapeake*, who was mortally wounded in the battle. Sometimes, this magnanimity seems to have been coupled with an existing naiveté. In July 1813, while patrolling off eastern Maine, *Boxer*'s boat captured a barge with more than a dozen men and four women on board. The boat was taken alongside *Boxer* and Blyth invited one of the American men and all four women into his cabin and interviewed them over coffee. Blyth took the Americans at their word that they were on an innocent passage and allowed them to proceed. As it turned out, the men were soldiers who had thrown their weapons and the only uniform items they possessed — the cockades on their hats — overboard. One of the women was actually the wife of the commander of the US fort at Eastport.

Although Blyth embodied many of the good qualities of Royal Naval officers, he also suffered from a number of their collective shortcomings. As Clausewitz wrote, "War is the realm of uncertainty: three quarters of the factors on which action in war is based are wrapped in a fog of greater or lesser uncertainty. A sensitive and discriminating judgment is called for; a skilled intelligence to scent out the truth." Blyth did not always display that judgment: like many of his brother officers, he believed that a ship could never have enough cannon and made the mistake of crowding *Boxer*'s decks with too many.[1] At some point, he even acquired two additional carronades in Halifax, making a total of twelve 18-pounder carronades and two 6-pounder long guns.

Blyth undoubtedly was brave, but he appears not to have possessed Hare's "sensitive and discriminating" instinct for sniffing out prizes and knowing when it was most appropriate to fight, withdraw, take a prize, or ransom it. And, while Blyth made some prize money, he seems to have let financial gain go to his head, augmenting his pay and prize money by expediting the smuggling trade that funnelled British manufactured

---

1   Guns were heavy and could affect a ship's stability and sailing qualities. They also cluttered the deck and made it more difficult to work the vessel. More guns also meant having to stretch the crew to man them, making the other cannon potentially less effective.

goods — such as textiles, blankets, silks, porcelain, tinware, and hardware — through Saint John into the United States, where they were in great demand. In Saint John, the goods would be loaded on board neutral vessels, often sailing under a Swedish or Spanish flag, which would then set forth for a US port, typically in Maine, where the goods could be legally landed if carried by a neutral ship. To expedite this illicit trade, US merchants paid Blyth to have *Boxer* protect these neutral ships from US privateers.

Depositions from Maine's Federal District Court indicate that some of Saint John's populace were familiar with *Boxer*'s role in this smuggling and were not very happy about it. Decades after the event, one smuggler confessed about the role *Boxer* played in protecting these operations. Writing in 1873, Charles Tappan states:

> At the commencement of our war with Great Britain in 1813, the United States had but few if any factories for the manufacture of woolen cloths and blankets, and the soldiers were clad in British cloths and slept under British blankets. It was understood no captures would be made of British goods owned by citizens of the United States, and many American merchants imported, via Halifax and St. John, N.B., their usual stock of goods. In 1813 I went with others in the "Swedish" brig *Margaretta* to St. John, N.B., and filled her with British goods, intending to take them to Bath, Maine, and enter them regularly and pay the lawful duties thereon. All we had to fear was American privateers; and we hired Capt. Blyth, of H.B.M. [His Britannic Majesty's] Brig *Boxer*, to convoy us to the mouth of the Kennebec river, for which service we gave him a bill of exchange on London for £100. We sailed in company, and in a thick fog, off Quoddy Head, the *Boxer* took us in tow. It was agreed that when we were about to enter the mouth of the [Kennebec] river two or three guns should

be fired over us, to have the appearance of trying to stop us, should any idle folks be looking on.

This letter reveals a startling level of complicity on Blyth's part. Not only did he accept a hefty fee to cover the smuggling trade, he even used *Boxer* to tow the smuggling ship. The sham firing on *Margaretta* as she "escaped" into the safety of the Kennebec River was all a part of a carefully orchestrated smuggling operation.

In fact, *Boxer*'s late summer tour took on the air of a yachting cruise. Little time seems to have been dedicated to gun drill. Instead, Blyth emphasized taking prizes and escorting smugglers. As summer waned, Blyth even took on board a passenger from Saint John's garrison, Lieutenant J.A. Allen of the 64th Regiment, who came along to recover his health. Although operating deep in US waters, Blyth became complacent. When his passenger and two midshipmen asked to go ashore on nearby Monhegan Island to shoot pigeons, he granted the request. The vessel's surgeon joined them to tend to a sick American civilian on the isolated island. Manning the oars of their boat were eight seamen, more than a tenth of *Boxer*'s complement of ratings. In the meantime, *Boxer* anchored off the mainland near Pemaquid Point, some miles away. Before long, however, on the morning of September 5, a strange sail was sighted. Blyth gave the order to hoist anchor and beat to quarters, and shaped a course to intercept the unknown vessel. She revealed herself to be an American warship, the U.S.S. *Enterprise*, and she shortly would bring *Boxer*'s wartime cruising to an end

The U.S.S. *Enterprise*

The exploits of the tiny *Bream* and larger *Boxer* had left Maine communities devastated. While they hoped to capture *Bream* with the few arms they had available, Maine's seafarers knew that *Boxer* was far too powerful to attack. Thus, in spring 1813, leaders in Maine seaports petitioned Washington for naval protection. Eventually, they were heard, and the national government sent the brig-of-war U.S.S. *Enterprise* "for the protection of the coast in the neighborhood." True to the low-intensity conflict model and Clausewitz, this was a political rather than a military decision. There was no strategic gain to be had in protecting the coasting trade of Maine and New Hampshire; rather, it was a political gesture to reassure locals that they had not been forgotten. In July and August, the *Enterprise* patrolled between Portland, Maine, and Portsmouth, New Hampshire. At the end of August, she arrived in Portland harbour in pursuit of a suspected British privateer.

Unlike *Boxer*, the *Enterprise* was a fairly old vessel, built at Baltimore in 1799. She was a veteran of the Quasi-War between the United States and France from 1799 to 1801 and after that had fought Barbary corsairs in the Mediterranean. Over the course of her career, the *Enterprise* had been rebuilt several times: originally rigged as a schooner, in 1812 she had been converted to a brig. In summer 1813, she had a crew of 102 and carried fourteen 18-pound carronades, and two long 9-pounders, making her somewhat more heavily armed than *Boxer* but much more heavily manned. Her commander since 1811 had been Johnston Blakely, who had a reputation for thoroughly drilling his crew at the brig's guns. The *Enterprise*'s mission was similar to that of *Boxer*: "protect the coasting trade...which has been so much interrupted by small cruisers of the enemy." Blakely had some success in suppressing or scattering several privateers from Nova Scotia and New Brunswick that had come to that coast, and had captured the tiny Halifax privateer *Fly*. A few days later, however, Blakely was ordered away from the *Enterprise* to take command of the brand new sloop-of-war *Wasp*, which was just being completed in Massachusetts, and was replaced by Lieutenant William Burrows.

Burrows had been born in Kensington, Pennsylvania, near Philadelphia, in 1785. He joined the US Navy as a midshipman at age fourteen and saw service in the Mediterranean against the Barbary corsairs. In early 1807, he was promoted to lieutenant and served on coastal gunboats for a time, then took furlough to sail on board a merchant vessel bound for China. Unfortunately for him, war broke out between Britain and the United States during his absence. On his ship's way back to the

United States, the Royal Navy captured her and took Burrows prisoner. Eventually exchanged, he returned to active duty in June 1813.

Burrows was considered something of an odd duck: although a fine sailor, he was moody and ambitious, terribly serious in demeanour, and thirsting for glory. He learned of *Boxer*'s presence when a fisherman arrived in Portland and reported seeing the brig fire at the *Margaretta* off the mouth of the Kennebec River. Burrows immediately got the *Enterprise* under way to intercept the British vessel. The wind was light and the tide was running against her, so the *Enterprise* had trouble getting out of Portland harbour. The crew manned sweeps to propel the vessel while locals used rowboats to tow the brig out past the fort on Spring Point. Once clear of land, she bore away for the mouth of the Kennebec.

Boxer versus the *Enterprise*

At dawn on September 5, the two brigs sighted each other, *Boxer* riding to anchor near Pemaquid Point while the *Enterprise* slowly approached in light airs. At 7:30 a.m., *Boxer* weighed anchor; shortly after that, she stopped a fishing boat by firing three shots, and Blyth asked the fishermen if they knew the identity of the approaching brig. The fishermen must have told him, since, a few minutes later, *Boxer* fired a cannon to challenge the American vessel, hoisted three ensigns, and headed directly for the *Enterprise*. Blyth must have sensed it would be a bloody battle, as he ordered the flags nailed to the mastheads.

Now notified about the intent of *Boxer*, and probably her exact identity, Burrows ordered the *Enterprise* to stand out to sea to allow room to manoeuvre. *Boxer* followed the *Enterprise* into open water in a slow-motion chase. The wind was light and for a time failed altogether, leaving both brigs becalmed. At 3:00 that afternoon, however, Burrows decided he had enough room to manoeuvre, and ordered the *Enterprise* to shorten sail and run down toward the British brig to engage.

Americans living on Maine's rocky coast flocked to the shore to watch the coming fight. Even as far away as Portland, spectators gathered at the base of the Observatory, a tower constructed to spot incoming shipping. Its keeper, Captain Lemuel Moody, climbed to the top and watched the two brigs manoeuvre through the morning, shouting any discoveries down to the anxious crowd below. By mid-afternoon, nothing seemed to be happening, and people began to leave. Then, at 3:00 p.m., Moody announced that he saw smoke from the guns but could not discern what was happening through his spyglass.

Both commanders determined to withhold fire until at very close range. For twenty minutes, the vessels slowly closed to within half a pistol shot. Then, at twenty minutes past three, *Boxer* fired a broadside and her crew gave three cheers. In a newspaper interview published in the *Portland Transcript* more than half a century later, John H. Aulick, who had been a midshipman aboard the *Enterprise*, claimed the British seamen mounted their guns to cheer, and while in this vulnerable position, the US vessel

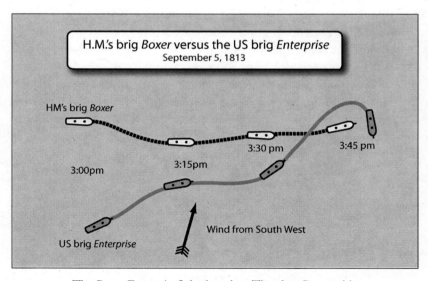

The *Boxer-Enterprise* fight, based on Theodore Roosevelt's interpretation of the battle. Joshua M. Smith

Flag from *Boxer*; note the five holes appearing at regular intervals on
the right edge, perhaps showing where it was spiked to the mast.
New York Public Library 112405

fired her port broadside, with devastating effect. The aged Aulick claimed,
"The British sailors after the action, said that the first broadside whipped
them." An eighteen-pound cannonball tore off Commander Blyth's left
arm and ripped open his gut, spilling out his intestines and covering his
face and the deck with his blood. Blyth, wounded so many times before in
his nation's service, died almost instantly.

A few minutes later, the *Enterprise*'s Lieutenant Burrows also fell,
mortally wounded by a cannon shot to the chest. As he lay bleeding on
deck, refusing to be carried below, he raised his head to demand that the
American flag never be struck.

Although both commanders were dead or dying, the fight continued
for forty-five minutes. Fifteen minutes into the battle, the *Enterprise* drew
ahead of the British brig, tacked and assumed a raking position, and fired
another devastating broadside. In a few minutes, *Boxer* was a complete
wreck, all of her braces and rigging shot away, her main topmast and top-
gallant mast hanging over the side, her fore- and mainmasts virtually gone,
three feet of water in her hold, and no surgeon to tend the wounded.

Not all of the *Enterprise*'s crew performed well. The brig's sailing

The BOXER and F

RIZE.   J. C. 1851

An American depiction
of the duel between
Boxer and the *Enterprise*.
McHS A00-4

master left his battle station and tried to hide behind the foremast to screen himself from *Boxer*'s gunfire, then advised Lieutenant Edward McCall to signal surrender by hauling down the ship's flag. The ship's clerk, perhaps panicked by seeing his commander shot, fled to the shot locker. Some of *Boxer*'s crew panicked as well, including the vessel's acting master's mate and three seamen, who all deserted their stations.

In contrast to these men, when the American lieutenant hailed the British vessel to know if she would surrender, one of *Boxer*'s crew leaped on a cannon, shook both fists at the Americans, and shouted "No, no, no!" along with some more colourful language that caused some laughter on board the *Enterprise*. Lieutenant David McCreary, who took command of *Boxer* after Blyth died, ordered the man down. Despite the bravado, McCreary ordered his crew to cease firing and hailed the *Enterprise* with his speaking trumpet to concede defeat. He could not signal this in the usual way by lowering his flag, however, because Blyth had ordered them nailed to the masts. John Aulick recalled the request to surrender as "Aint you going to give quarter, we have surrendered."

A party from the *Enterprise* boarded the shattered British brig and took sixty-four prisoners, seventeen of them wounded. *Boxer*'s crew had thrown a number of their dead overboard, making it unclear at first just how many died. Blyth's sword was picked up and brought to the quarterdeck of the *Enterprise*, where the wounded Burrows still lay. When the sword was presented, he reportedly clasped his hands and said, "I am satisfied, I die contented." Only then did he consent to be taken below. The American brig had two killed and twelve wounded, including Burrows, who died that night.

The next morning, the two vessels entered Portland harbour, the *Enterprise* leading the way, and came directly to a wharf, where anybody who wished was allowed to come on board. One of the curious, a Portland schoolteacher, boarded *Boxer* to find the deck scarred by shot, spattered with blood, and littered with weapons dropped during the fight, and Blyth's corpse still lying on the quarterdeck. Portland's discreet smuggling merchants arranged for someone to go on board and dispose of any incriminating evidence of their activities, especially the bill of exchange, which was found in Blyth's breeches pocket. Smugglers but not without honour, they replaced the incriminating piece of paper with $500 in specie, presumably for the benefit of Blyth's widow.

Spectators agreed that, while the American vessel was damaged, the British ship presented a grim scene. A US naval officer expressed his amazement at how little the American brig had suffered, and how damaged the British brig was:

> The *Enterprize* has but one 18 pound shot in her hull, one in her mainmast, and one in her foremast; her sails are much cut with grapeshot, and there are a great number of grape lodged in her sides, but no injury done by them. The *Boxer* has eighteen or twenty 18 pound shot in her hull, most of them at the water's edge; several stands of 18 pound grape stick in her side, and such a quantity of small grape that I do not undertake to count them. Her masts, sails and spars are literally cut to pieces, several of her guns are dismounted and unfit for service; her topgallant forecastle nearly taken off by the shot; her boats cut to pieces, and her quarters injured in proportion. To give you an idea of the quantity of shot about her, I inform you that I counted in her mainmast alone, three 18 pound shot holes, 18 large grape shot holes, 16 musket ball holes, and a large number of smaller shot holes.

A Funeral

The Americans incarcerated *Boxer*'s crew in Fort Preble in Portland. A few escaped, but the garrison quickly rounded them up. The officers were paroled on their honour not to escape and allowed to rent rooms in a hotel. With little to do, they toured about Portland, including visiting the Observatory and using the spyglass to take in the view. Once someone realized that the view included the harbour forts, which were preparing for an anticipated attack, this practice was stopped. After a few days, *Boxer*'s crew was taken to a prison ship in Salem, Massachusetts, while the officers travelled to Boston to await exchange. Before they left, there was one matter left to attend to: their commander's burial.

Funeral ceremonies for the two fallen naval commanders were held jointly in Portland, and they were truly a spectacular event — a piece of street theatre carefully orchestrated to reinforce such social ideals as bravery in combat, gallantry toward the enemy, and respect for the fallen. The relative youthfulness of the two officers (Blyth was twenty-nine, Burrows twenty-eight) seems to have added to the maudlin tone of their funeral preparations. On Wednesday, September 8, the preparations were complete. All businesses were closed, flags flown at half-staff, and church bells tolled at intervals. A procession of officials and uniformed militia units marched to the waterfront to receive the corpses of the two officers, which were landed by barges to the musical accompaniment of a band and cannon salutes from both the *Enterprise* and *Boxer*. Once ashore, prominent locals took up positions as pallbearers, with the officers and crew of the two vessels following the remains of their respective former commanders. Anybody with any sort of social status was in the procession: selectmen, clergy, military and naval officers, judges, congressmen, sea captains, and even bank officers. The masses, many of whom had travelled from the country to witness the event, watched from the side or crowded windows and rooftops to observe the grandest funeral procession Portland had ever seen. Other than the official guns, bells, and funeral dirges, a respectful quiet overcame the crowd.

In the aftermath of the battle, the crew of the *Enterprise* was publicly lauded and feasted before hoisting anchor and leaving. The one exception was Midshipman Kerwin Waters, who had been badly wounded in the battle and could not be moved; he lingered on for more than a year before dying. *Boxer*'s surgeon, who had rejoined the ship's company after being arrested by local militia on Monhegan Island, treated the wounded from both vessels in Portland until they were fit to be moved. The remainder of *Boxer*'s crew went into captivity in Massachusetts; some of them eventually faced a court martial for poor conduct during the battle.

For Americans, the defeat of *Boxer* was a chance to crow, and they have continued to do so ever since. Scots-born US political cartoonist

Boxer's medicine cabinet; the brig's surgeon treated the wounded from both sides after the battle. McHS 1764

Yankee propaganda, circa late 1813; while the *Boxer-Enterprise* duel was only a minor affair, American propagandists attempted to portray it as a major event. LC-USZCN4-217

William Charles attempted to inflate the importance of the *Boxer-Enterprise* duel in a cartoon labelled "A boxing match, or another bloody nose for John Bull." In it, Charles portrays George III with his nose gushing blood and eye blackened, saying, "Stop Stop Stop Brother Jonathan, or I shall fall with the loss of blood — I thought to have been too heavy for you — But I must acknowledge your superior skill — Two blows to my one! — And so well directed too! Mercy, mercy on me, how does this happen!!!" On the right, his opponent James Madison says, "Ha-Ah Johnny! you thought yourself a Boxer did you! — I'll let you know we are an Enterpriseing Nation and ready to meet you with equal force any day." In the background the two vessels are engaged in battle.

Charles's cartoon, however, is a clumsy effort at best. By late 1813, the Royal Navy had seized control of the entire US coastline with a close blockade, and the US oceanic fleet was largely trapped in harbour. After defeating *Boxer*, the *Enterprise* never returned to the Gulf of Maine. Except for privateers, which by the end of 1813 had been reduced to a mere nuisance, the British completely dominated these waters.

Why, however, had the *Enterprise* prevailed over *Boxer*? British naval pride suffered only a small wound by the loss, but much ink was spilled analyzing the event. Some criticized Blyth for nailing his colours to the mast as it indicated he "either doubted his own fortitude, or that of his associates," but given Blyth's combat record and the behaviour of the overwhelming majority of *Boxer*'s crew, this seems unlikely. He nevertheless was blamed for this "barbarous practice" because it had exposed his men to unnecessary danger after they ceased resisting. A London newspaper called this action "always a most foolish and perilous boast in advance."

A more serious accusation was that the *Enterprise* had handled her guns much better. A London newspaper noted, "The fact seems to be but too clearly established that the Americans have *some superior mode of firing*, and we can not be too anxiously employed in discovering to what circumstances that superiority is owing." The naval historian William James writes that "the *Boxer*'s men appear to have known very little what use to make of their guns," while the Americans "had evidently been well practiced" at gunnery. James calls the duel "a very creditable affair to the Americans," but also notes "the American vessel was doubly superior in crew, better formed in every respect, nearly a third larger, and constructed ... of much stouter scantling."

Despite the boasting and complaining on both sides, the *Boxer-Enterprise* duel did nothing to change the outcome of the war. The Royal Navy remained in firm control of the Bay of Fundy and almost the entire US eastern seaboard for the remainder of the war. Locally, its impact was more emotional than strategic, especially among the British seamen and officers in Saint John, including those of the tiny schooner *Bream*.

Epilogue

As rumours about *Boxer*'s battle trickled back to Saint John, the city's newspapers began to suspect the worst had happened. When the news finally arrived more than a week after the action, it was met with shock and disbelief. Somehow the crew of *Bream* caught wind of some criticism of the Royal Navy. Anxious to vindicate British naval honour, *Bream*'s crew wrote a letter to her commander stating their wish to challenge the *Enterprise* to a one-on-one duel:

His Majesty's Schr. *Bream*, Sept. 18th, 1813.

Dear Sir,

It is the request of the Schooner's Company that you have the honor to command, to request the Commodore to allow us to have another cruise to the Westward, being upbraided with Cowardice in the British Navy, (on Shore), respecting the action of the *Boxer*.

It is the, wish, of the Schooner's Crew, provided that we can muster Sixty hands, to challenge, the *Enterprise* to meet us in the same place she did the *Boxer*. You may think this a piece of impudence, to challenge a vessel of so much superior force, but we think that we can "lay her aboard," and carry her with that compliment of men; and it is for you to judge whether you think that there is a Coward among the Crew that, you have the honor to command.

Dear Sir, it is our most ardent wish to have this trial: knowing your abilities, and the rest of the Officers, that; we shall have the pleasure of bringing the *Enterprise* into Saint John; and hope, and know as long as you have the pleasure to command, that we are certain that she will never be given up cowardly . . . and it is the wish of your servants to show their loyalty to their King and Country, and are never afraid to bleed in its cause.

> (Signed) ALL HANDS,
> The Crew of H. M. Schr. *Bream*
> To Lieutenant Charles Hare,
> Commander.

This remarkable letter indicates that the concept of bravery, or at least fear of being labelled a coward, was a compelling factor in promoting crew loyalty and fighting spirit. Years later, Hare wrote that "at the period [the letter] was received it afforded me not a little gratification, and evinces the good humor and fighting mood the crew (I had the honor to command, as they so kindly and proudly remind me of) were kept in."

By late 1813, the British navy began to reallocate ships away from fighting Napoleon to the North American war. In the Bay of Fundy and Gulf of Maine region, this was most apparent in the increasing numbers of sloops-of-war that began to appear. Either ship or brig rigged,[1] these vessels were more heavily armed and manned than *Brunswicker*, *Bream*, or *Boxer* and proved to be ideal for convoying merchant vessels, patrolling against privateers, and blockading the entire length of the Maine coast. Hare benefited

---

1   Ship rigged refers to a three-masted vessel with a series of square sails on each mast. A brig was a two-masted vessel with square sails.

from this shift to larger vessels. In winter 1814, Commodore Henry Le Fleming Senhouse briefly gave him command of the sloop-of-war *Manly* after her regular crew marched overland along the iced-over St. John River to the Great Lakes fleet in Upper Canada via Montreal.

Hare also participated in bigger operations in the Bay of Fundy/Gulf of Maine region. On July 11, 1814, Admiral Sir Thomas M. Hardy captured the town of Eastport. His flagship, the seventy-four gun *Ramillies*, was the first ship-of-the-line to enter the Bay of Fundy during the entire war. Hare piloted *Ramillies* through Passamaquoddy Bay's complex channels, putting his knowledge and skills to work for an invasion fleet instead of a tiny schooner. Accompanying *Ramillies* was the sloop *Martin*, the brig *Borer,* Hare's old command *Bream,* the bombship *Terror,* and several transports loaded with troops. Faced with this overwhelming force, the American garrison at Fort Sullivan surrendered without firing a shot. In September, the towns of Castine and Machias also fell to invasion fleets, leaving all of the Maine coast east of the Penobscot River in British hands. In both instances, Hare acted as a pilot for the invading forces. But his time in the region was almost over: the navy had different plans for the young lieutenant.

When Hare left the Bay of Fundy for duty elsewhere, the leading merchants, shipowners, and most important citizens of Saint John — including the mayor, members of the provincial council, and the chamber of commerce — thanked him by writing a letter to Sir John B. Warren, commander-in-chief of the Royal Navy's North American station, expressing their appreciation for the protection he offered and asking that he remain there. Despite their protests, Hare left to take command of the brigantine *Pictou*, carrying dispatches to various units and even to England. He liked this duty because it gave him the chance to capture American ships, but he came across only one brig laden with salt, which he ransomed for £750. With that final incident, which took place on January 5, 1815, his war ended. In fact, the peace treaty had been signed on Christmas Eve 1814.

Fates of the Ships and Their Commanders

The story of the three British ships considered here — *Brunswicker*, *Bream*, and *Boxer* — does not end with the cessation of hostilities with the United States.

The fates of *Brunswicker* and her commander, James Reed, were closely linked to Saint John's waterfront. In early summer 1815, the ship was auctioned off by Vice-Admiralty Court officers. A crier walked the streets of Saint John, ringing a bell and trying to excite interest in the vessel's sale. On July 4, 1815, she sold for a paltry £693 to Noah Disbrow of Saint John, an up-and-coming merchant captain. The expense of keeping the ship was just over £632, leaving the province £61 in debt against operating expenses of £771 as well as the initial purchase price of £1250, for a total loss of £1311. *Brunswicker*'s eventual disposition is unknown.

James Reed continued to serve against the Americans after *Brunswicker* was laid up in spring 1813. That autumn he took command of the 38-ton sloop *Hare* for a single cruise in New England waters. *Hare* was probably named after Charles Hare, given the young lieutenant's popularity in Saint John and the fact that the vessel had previously been the American privateer *Wasp*, which *Bream* had captured. *Bream*'s logbook also recorded that Reed piloted the schooner on occasion; given their common interests, he and Hare might well have struck up a friendship. After British forces captured the town of Castine in 1814, Reed became master of the 160-ton schooner *Snap Dragon*, another captured American privateer. The *Snap Dragon* sailed between Castine and Saint John at least three times, carrying British goods to the occupied port and returning to Saint John with American flour, during which time the vessel was unsuccessfully attacked by US vessels at least twice. After the war, Reed resumed his career as a civilian mariner and became a branch pilot of the port of Saint John. Eventually, the colony appointed him lighthouse keeper on Partridge Island. He died on the island at age 51 on Sunday, September 30, 1835, when he fell from a precipice. He was buried with Masonic and militia honours in the Episcopal churchyard near Courtenay Bay.

Bream continued to sail in New Brunswick waters through summer

Site of James Reed's death: Partridge Island and Saint John harbour, circa 1835.
Drawing and lithograph by Mary G. Hall. LAC C-008744

1814, but her luck seems to have dried up after Hare left. When *Bream*'s barges chased a boatload of US soldiers ashore at Lubec in late April 1814, the Americans formed up and chased off the barges with volleys of small-arms fire. The next month, when *Bream*'s twelve-oared barge crewed by a midshipman and six men approached the beached lumber schooner *William & John* in Pigeon Hill Bay, the Yankee crew opened a devastating fire, and two of the barge's crew were shot dead and two wounded, one mortally. The midshipman wisely surrendered to the lumber schooner's master. The commander of *Bream*, anxious to recover his midshipman and sailors, entered into negotiations with the master, ultimately granting him twenty-five dollars in cash for each returned prisoner, the return of two American prisoners, a chebacco boat and its cargo worth seven hundred dollars, and the twelve-oared barge and all its weapons, including a swivel gun. It was a humiliating example of the biter being bit.

If *Bream* took any more prizes, they are not recorded in the Halifax Vice-Admiralty Court records. After assisting in the occupation of Moose Island in July 1814, *Bream* left for Chesapeake Bay where it served until the end of the war. When peace came, the hard-used little vessel returned to Bermuda, where she had been built. On arrival she was taken out of service and broken up two years later.

Bream's most influential commander, Charles Hare, returned to Saint John and lived out his days in New Brunswick with his wife and growing family, six of whom survived infancy. In 1816, Edward Griffith recommended that Hare apply to command a revenue cutter, but Hare either could not find such a position or eschewed it for work on board merchant vessels. He worked for a number of Saint John merchants, including the firm of John Ward and Sons, his vessels earning a fine reputation for both safety and speed — by 1839, he had crossed the Atlantic ninety-eight times without loss or accident. As master of the ship *Waterloo* of almost four hundred tons burthen, he landed four cargoes from Saint John to Liverpool in thirteen months. As master of the brig *Ward* (of which he was part owner), he sailed from Saint John to Liverpool and back in a mere seventy-two days. It was not always easy sailing. On one occasion, he nearly hit an iceberg, but his vigilance and his practice of using a thermometer to determine when ice was nearby saved the *Ward* from disaster. Hare, in fact, became somewhat of a celebrated navigator, widely consulted for such matters as digging a canal across the Chignecto Isthmus, building a lighthouse on Grand Manan, the best route between New Brunswick and Britain, and even determining the boundaries of the Gulf Stream.

Hare's lack of promotion was all too common in the Royal Navy after 1815. As N.A.M. Rodger describes in *The Command of the Ocean*, the Admiralty had recruited so many officers during the Napoleonic Wars that, with peace and a much reduced navy, it could find no employment for many of them. Nonetheless, Hare campaigned for promotion in 1815, 1819, 1829, and again in 1839. By 1842, Admiral Sir Jahleel Brenton was forced to tell his old midshipman that, though he wished him well, he could not get a promotion even for his own son-in-law, who had languished as a lieutenant for twenty-eight years. In 1848, Hare published a pamphlet advocating for promotion, *Testimonials and Memorials of the Services of Lieut. Charles Hare, of the Royal Navy*. But its doleful subtitle, *37 Years a Lieutenant*, indicated the futility of his cause, as did a passage on the cover that read "EXHIBITING Another painful proof of the great injustice done to a large and meritorious body of Naval Officers, in being denied that promotion to which their services entitle them; but to which, superior political or family influence almost daily advances their juniors, both in years and rank." Hare lacked the patronage to advance in rank, a fate common among naval officers.

Hare died in Saint John in 1859, still a lieutenant. He was predeceased by his son William, who died when the British troopship *Birkenhead* wrecked on the south African coast in 1852. In a curious coincidence, *Birkenhead* originally had been called *Vulcan*, the same name as that of the ship his grandfather had commanded at Toulon in 1793. News of William's death precipitated his mother's death in 1853, as is attested to by her grave marker at Trinity Church's burial ground in Saint John.

After her capture, *Boxer* met a curious fate. For a time, she was used as a floating battery to defend Portland against an anticipated attack. Ultimately, the US Navy did not take her into service, and the vessel was sold at auction for $5,600 to a Portland merchant named Thomas Merrill, Jr. Her ten 18-pound carronades and two 6-pound cannon were sold separately, as were her thirty-six tons of "kentlege" (iron ballast) and other items on board for a total of $9,755 (see Appendix Table 2 for a complete inventory). The heirs of Captain Burrows received $1,115 in prize money, while the seamen of the *Enterprise* got a mere $55. With the war over, *Boxer* went into the merchant service under the command of Captain William McLellan, sailing out of Portland for many years in the West Indies trade. Naval historian William James sniffs that this commerce was the only service for which the brig had ever been calculated.

Samuel Blyth, of course, died in battle and was buried alongside Lieutenant Burrows in the Eastern Cemetery in Portland, Maine (they

Watercolour of *Boxer* as a US merchant ship after 1814. McHS 2005.500.060

were joined by Midshipman Kerwin Waters when he died in 1815). The officers and crew of *Boxer* arranged for Blyth's grave marker before they left Portland. No less than Henry Wordsworth Longfellow referenced both the battle and the graves in the poem "My Lost Youth":

> I remember the sea-fight far away,
> How it thundered o'er the tide!
> And the dead captains, as they lay
> In their graves, o'erlooking the tranquil bay
> Where they in battle died.
> And the sound of that mournful song
> Goes through me with a thrill:
> "A boy's will is the wind's will,
> And the thoughts of youth are long, long thoughts.

The graves of Blyth and Burrows in Eastern Cemetery, Portland, Maine.
LC D4-71502

Conclusion

Après la guerre

The ships that guarded New Brunswick during the War of 1812 were not glamorous vessels with famous names; they were small, uncomfortable craft engaged in tedious yet dangerous duties on the treacherous Bay of Fundy. While New Brunswick never produced a seaman to rival the fictional Horatio Hornblower or Jack Aubrey, its mariners served in conjunction with others from around the British Empire and beyond. In so doing, they connected themselves with the larger world, whether the parlours of Jane Austen's novels or the wardrooms of Frederick Marryat's works. Some Royal Navy veterans, such as Charles Hare, even settled in New Brunswick's ports, further connecting the colony to a bustling and growing empire.

The Royal Navy remained a presence in New Brunswick until Confederation in 1867. Its role continued to be largely that of a floating constabulary, chasing American fishermen out of British waters, pursuing smugglers, and arresting mutineers on commercial vessels. The advent of steam technology did not really change that role significantly. When war or invasion threatened, as during the so-called Aroostook War, the US Civil War, or the Fenian Crisis of 1866, Saint John's harbour became crowded with British men-of-war and troop transports. Saint John might never have been the important naval base Halifax was, but as the leading commercial and industrial centre of the Bay of Fundy, it was an important strategic asset. To this day, Saint John remains the province's most important harbour, and it is especially fitting that the Canadian Navy's reserve unit in Saint John, H.M.C.S. *Brunswicker*, is named in honour of one of the tiny craft that defended the region during the War of 1812.

The "Capture of *Snap Dragon*" in June 1814. By Irwin John Bevan.
Mariner's Museum QW311

Appendix 1

Prizes Captured by
H.M. Schooner *Bream*, 1812-1813

PRIZE NAME	RIG	TONS	MASTER	ROUTE	DATE CAPTURED	CARGO	LOCATION
Pythagoras (privateer)	sloop	42	Libby, Cyrus	cruising from Saco, ME	August 9, 1812		off Ragged Islands, NS just east of Shelburne
Defiance	schooner	113	Altham, T.	Castine, ME to Boston	March 31, 1813	cord-wood	off Townshend, ME
Neptune	schooner	98	Mills, B.	Fox Island, ME to Boston	March 31, 1813	timber, cord-wood	off Townshend, ME
Lark	sloop	70	Dodge, J.	Portsmouth, NH to Penobscot, ME	April 19, 1813	corn, cotton, molasses, 2 wheel-barrows	between Monhegan & Towns-hend, ME
Susannah	sloop	89	Marshal, L.	Deer Isle, ME to Boston	April 20, 1813	cord-wood	2 leagues off Mon-hegan, ME
Semerimes	sloop	85	Loop, D.	Pleasant River, ME to Boston	April 23, 1813	timber, cord-wood	off Monhegan, ME

PRIZE NAME	RIG	TONS	MASTER	ROUTE	DATE CAPTURED	CARGO	LOCATION
Branch	schooner	78	Lukins, H.	Boston to Deer Island, ME	April 26, 1813	ballast	off Monhegan, ME
Pilgrim	boat	25	Brooks, Ant'y	Boston to Eastport, ME	April 27, 1813	gin, tobacco, flour, etc.	off West Quoddy Head, ME
Sally	schooner	74	Cousins, J.	Eastport, ME to Boston	May 13, 1813	plaister, salt, fish	off Little River, ME
Jefferson	schooner	99	Colcord, J.	Boston to Prospect, ME	July 12, 1813	ballast	near Georges Island, ME
Triton	schooner	122	McFarlane, Geo.	St. Thomas, VI to Kennebec, ME	July 14, 1813	45 punch-eons rum & 6 hogs-heads molasses	20 miles off Portland, ME
Wasp (privateer)	sloop	40	Irvin, E.A.	cruising from Salem, MA	August 8, 1813		near Brier Island, NS, in the Bay of Fundy

Sources: Contemporary newspaper accounts and prize records of the Vice-Admiralty Court, Halifax.

Inventory of Items Sold from
H.M. Brig *Boxer*, November 1813*

NOVEMBER 12, 1813, SALE AT AUCTION ON A/C OF T. G. THORNTON ESQ. MARSHALL	PRICE (US $)
No. 1 & 2 Brig *Boxer* and appurtenances Thos. Merrill Jr.	$5,600.00
3 10- 18" Carronades Do	800.00
4 2 6' Cannon Wm. Sturgis	131.00
5 Lot muskets, pistols, swords &c T. Fletcher	364.00
6 " magazine Furniture T. Merrill Jr.	81.00
7 " musket ball cartridges Do	72.00
8 " 18" cartridges Do	119.00
9 " 7 & part Casks powder Do	161.00
10 " Cabin Furniture T. Fletcher	165.00
11 " Chairs Carpets & curtains T. Collins Jr	79.00
12 " Shoes, hats, & trowsers Th. Merrill Jr	60.00
13 Box 50 feet 7 by 9 glass JW. Quincy	7.50
14 Lot water casks & breakers R. Morton	230.00
15 1 Case Charts D. Stackpole	47.00
16 70 Flags & signals Th. Merrill Jr	145.00
17 Kentledge* Tons 36.00 [crossed out] Th. J. Chew @ 38	1368.00
18 6 part bbls Rum 104/ Gals M & W Harris @1.90	198.55
19 1 Bbl. Oatmeal J. Cross Jr	5.25

NOVEMBER 12, 1813, SALE AT AUCTION ON A/C OF T. G. THORNTON ESQ. MARSHALL	PRICE (US $)
20 4 Do Pease W. Sturgis @3.25	13.00
21 2 Do Flour J. Steel @11.	22.00
22 2 Do Beef J. & A Carter @8.25	16.50
23 4 Do Pork W. Sturgis @14.25	57.00
24 2 half bbls do J. Steel @5.	10.00
25 1 Bbl. Butter T. Collins Jr	14.25
26 1 Cask & bag cocoa J. Steel	6.25
27 Part cask malaga wine W. Sturgis	19.25
28 Do box chocolate J. Steel	5.25
30 [sic] Bag Coffee J Cross Jr	17.00
31 4 Small bags sugar & 2 raisins Do	40.00
32 13 Bags Bread JW. Quincy	32.00
33 3 Do Pease J & A Carter	3.50
34 2 part Kegs oil J. Steel	
	9896.30
Sundry articles taken for Brig *Rattlesnake* S. Storer Esq	1184 .25
Do""""*Enterprise* Do	556.14
Do"""""Do	37.50
	1,777.89
	$11,674.19

Portland, November 15, 1813

Note: "Do" means Ditto, or "the same as above."
Source: Maine Historical Society.

Acknowledgements

Books are generally collaborative projects, and this one is no exception. Professor Marc Milner of the University of New Brunswick urged me to take on this book as part of the New Brunswick Military Heritage Project. I was delighted to do so, as it meshed neatly with research already completed and various projects about the War of 1812 era already under way. My fondest wish is that someone will pick up this book and be inspired to conduct further research into this little-known arena of a conflict that continues to shape North American relations.

Canadian colleagues who assisted with research during a stay in Ottawa in 2001-2002 include independent scholar Faye Kert, Professor Julian Gwyn of the University of Ottawa, and Timothy Dubé of the National Archives of Canada. New Brunswick's cultural heritage agencies were extremely helpful in responding to my research requests: I thank Gary Hughes, Janet Bishop, and Jennifer Longon of the New Brunswick Museum in Saint John and Heather Lyons of the Provincial Archives of New Brunswick in Fredericton for their efforts. Kelly Chaves, an American, is a doctoral candidate at the University of New Brunswick; she very kindly looked through early drafts and made numerous helpful suggestions. Brent Wilson also contributed enormously by editing the manuscript, coordinating e-mail, answering questions, finding illustrations, and undertaking myriad other tasks necessary to the publication of this work.

The greatest contribution was made by the descendants of Charles Hare, who features so prominently in the third chapter. Barbara Hare very kindly took the time to copy papers in her family's possession and gave permission to publish photographs of family heirlooms. The photographs were taken by her son, Jeffrey Hare. Without her help, this would have been a much lesser work.

On the US side of the border, Captain Michael Rutstein, owner and master of the re-created Salem privateer *Fame*, very kindly shared his extensive research and images of his beautiful schooner. The staff of the Schuyler Otis Bland Library at the US Merchant Marine Academy was generous in assisting me; in particular, the inter-library loan efforts of Mr. Donald Gill were above and beyond the call of duty. My friends and colleagues at the US Merchant Marine Academy assisted me more than they know. John Guerin and Bernard Gelman brought new light to this project; likewise Steve Gitlin and Ed Schuldner always delivered in a timely manner, as did George Cliff despite pressing business elsewhere. Georgia Durant's enduring support has taken me (and several other scholars) down roads unthinkable without her kind assistance.

Research occasionally required help outside North America. Eric Schoutens of the Douanes Impériales Association in the Netherlands provided some tips and important information that took this book in new directions. My friends and colleagues on Marhst-L, an international electronic discussion group sponsored and administered by the Marine Museum of the Great Lakes with the assistance of Queen's University at Kingston, Ontario, were a great help.

Thanks also to the staff at Goose Lane Editions, in particular Angela Williams and Jaye Haworth, and to Barry Norris for his careful editing.

Finally, I thank my wife Jea and daughter Dorothea for their continued patience as their husband and father set forth on yet another writing project. As usual, any errors are my own, and I take full responsibility for them.

Selected Bibliography

Anonymous. "The Affair of the *Enterprise* and *Boxer*." Portland Transcript, 1885(?), newspaper clipping in Maine Historical Society Coll. 442, "Maine Historical Manuscripts," volume 6, p. 89.

Graves, Donald E., ed. *Merry Hearts Make Light Days: The War of 1812 Journals of Lieutenant John Le Couteur, 104th Foot*. Ottawa: Carleton University Press, 1993.

Gwyn, Julian. *Ashore and Afloat: The British Navy and the Halifax Naval Yard before 1820*. Ottawa: University of Ottawa Press, 2004.

_____. *Frigates and Foremasts: The North American Squadron in Nova Scotia Waters, 1745-1815*. Studies in Canadian Military History 4. Vancouver: University of British Columbia Press, 2003.

_____. "The Halifax Naval Yard and Mast Contractors, 1775-1815." *Northern Mariner* 11 (4, 2001): 1-25.

Hannay, James. *History of New Brunswick*. Saint John, NB: J.A. Bowes, 1909.

Hare, Charles. *Testimonials and Memorials of the Services of Lieut. Charles Hare, of the Royal Navy, 37 Years a Lieutenant*. Saint John, NB: [s.n.], 1848.

Hubley, Martin. "Mass Desertion and Mutiny — The Case of HM Brig *Columbine*." Halifax, NS: Maritime Museum of the Atlantic.

Available online at http://museum.gov.ns.ca/mma/research/web/mutiny.html#_ftnref3; last accessed August 1, 2010.

Kert, Faye. *Prize and Prejudice: Privateering and Naval Prize in Atlantic Canada in the War of 1812*. Research in Maritime History 11. St. John's, NL: International Maritime Economic History Association, 1997.

_____. *Trimming Yankee Sails: Pirates and Privateers of New Brunswick*. New Brunswick Military Heritage Series 6. Fredericton, NB: Goose Lane Editions and New Brunswick Military Heritage Project, 2005.

Kindred, Sheila Johnson. "Charles Austen: Prize Chaser and Prize Taker on the North American Station, 1805-1808." *Persuasions: The Jane Austen Journal* 26 (2004): 188-194.

Lavery, Brian. *Nelson's Navy: The Ships, Men and Organization, 1793-1815*. Annapolis, MD: Naval Institute Press, 1989; reprint 1995.

Lyon, David. *The Sailing Navy List: All the Ships of the Royal Navy: Built, Purchased and Captured, 1688-1860*. London: Conway Maritime Press, 1993.

MacNutt, W. Stewart. *New Brunswick, a History: 1784-1867*. Toronto: Macmillan of Canada, 1984.

McKee, Christopher. *A Gentlemanly and Honorable Profession: The Creation of the US Naval Officer Corps, 1794-1815*. Annapolis, MD: Naval Institute Press, 1991.

Mercer, Keith. "Northern Exposure: Resistance to Naval Impressment in British North America, 1775-1815." *Canadian Historical Review* 91 (2, 2010): 199-232.

New Brunswick. Provincial Archives of New Brunswick. *Legislative Assembly: Sessional Records* (RS24). Available online at http://archives.gnb.ca/APPS/GovRecs/RS24/?culture=en-CA.

Picking, Sherwood. *Sea Fight Off Monhegan: Enterprise and Boxer*. Portland, ME: Machigonne Press, 1941.

Raikes, Henry. *Memoir of the Life and Services of Vice-Admiral Sir Jahleel Brenton, Baronet, K.C.B.* London: Hatchard and Son [etc.], 1846.

Rodger, N.A.M. *The Command of the Ocean: A Naval History of Britain, 1649-1815*. New York: W.W. Norton, 2005.

Rogers, Nicholas. *The Press Gang: Naval Impressment and Its Opponents in Georgian Britain*. London: Continuum, 2007.

Rutstein, Michael. *Fame: The Salem Privateer*. Essex, MA: Pennant Enterprises, 2002.

Sarty, Roger, and Doug Knight. *Saint John Fortifications, 1630-1956*. New Brunswick Military Heritage Series 1. Fredericton, NB: Goose Lane Editions and New Brunswick Military Heritage Project, 2003.

Smith, Joshua M. *Blockhouse & Battery: A History of Fort Edgecomb*. Edgecomb, ME.: Friends of Fort Edgecomb, 2009.

_____. *Borderland Smuggling: Patriots, Loyalists, and Illicit Trade in the Northeast, 1783-1820*. Gainesville, FL: University Press of Florida, 2006.

Snider, C.H.J. *Under the Red Jack; Privateers of the Maritime Provinces of Canada in the War of 1812*. London: M. Hopkinson, 1928.

Wells, William R. "US Revenue Cutters Captured in the War of 1812." *American Neptune* 58 (3, 1998): 225-241.

Zimmerman, David. *Coastal Fort: A History of Fort Sullivan, Eastport, Maine*. Eastport, ME: Border Historical Society, 1984.

Photo Credits

The drawing on page 12 (Isaac Erb Fonds: P11-57) appears courtesy of the Provincial Archives of New Brunswick (PANB). The painting on page 19 appears courtesy of the National Archives of Canada (NAC). The sketch on page 20 appears courtesy of the Florida Center for Institutional Technology. The drawing on page 23 (1146965), the painting on page 64 (478519), the drawing on page 71 (1199102), and the flag on page 83 (112405) appear courtesy of the Miriam & Ira D. Wallach Division of Art, Prints and Photographs, New York Public Library. The maps on pages 26, 43, 53 (based on W.O. 55/860, p. 422), 61, and 82 appear courtesy of Joshua M. Smith. The paintings on page 30 (QW 280), 54, and 104 (QW311) appear courtesy of the Mariners' Museum (MM). The painting on page 34 appears courtesy of Captain Michael Rutstein at http://www.schoonerfame.com. The chart on page 37 appears courtesy of the National Archives and Records Administration (NARA) RG21, "Records of the District Courts of the United States, Southern District of New York. The drawing on page 40 (H261 2945), the cartoon on page 90 (USZCN4-217), and the photo on page 101 appear courtesy of the Library of Congress (LC). The drawing on page 46 (W6725) appears courtesy of the New Brunswick Museum (NBM). The paintings on pages 48 (C-016386), 51 (C-011221), and 97 (C-008744) appear courtesy of Library and Archives Canada (LAC). The drawing on page 57 appears courtesy of Edward William Cooke (artist) in *Ships & Ways of Other Days* by E. Keble Chatterton (London: Sidgwick and Jackson, Ltd., 1913). The drawing on page 62 appears courtesy of Snider, *Under the Red Jack*. The painting on page 65, the drawing on page 66, and the uniform on page 68 appear courtesy of the Hare Family. The drawings on page 74 (OJ359.09N227V32), 84-85 (A00-4), the photo on page 89

(1764), and the painting on page 100 (2005.500.060) appear courtesy of Maine Historical Society (MeHS). All illustrative material is reproduced by permission.

Index

A

Acasta 38
Active 38, 105
Actress 38
África 39
Alexander 60
Allen, Lieutenant J.A. 79
Altham, T. 105
American Revolution 16, 33, 41, 65
Amphion 67
Annapolis, NS 38
Argus 38
Army, British
    64th Regiment 79
    104th (New Brunswick) Regiment
       of Foot 35
Aroostook War 103
Aulick, John H. 82, 86
Austen, Charles 15
Austen, Jane 15, 103

B

Badger, H.M. Brig 75
Bagley, Samuel 49, 50
Bailey's Mistake ME 38
Baltimore MD 80
Bandon, Daniel 50
Barbados, H.M.S. 69
Barry, John 40-41
Bass Harbor ME 60
Bath ME 78
Battle of Trafalgar 13, 15, 16, 19, 69

Bay of Fundy 9, 10, 15, 16, 17, 18, 19,
    26, 27, 28, 29, 31, 32, 33, 34, 35, 36,
    38, 39, 41, 44, 46, 55, 58, 61, 62,
    63, 69, 70, 72, 75, 91, 94, 95, 103,
    104, 106
Beaver Harbour NB 32
Belvedira 39
Bermuda 56, 98
Berry, Samuel 50
Betsy 60
Bevan, Irwin John 30, 104
Birkenhead, H.M.S. 99
Black, John 69
Black, William 69
Blakely, Captain Johnston 80
Blenheim, H.M.S. 9
Bliss, Chief Justice Jonathan 47
Blyth, Captain Samuel 75-79, 81, 83,
    86-88, 91, 99, 101
Boothbay ME 59, 60, 62
Borer, H.M. Brig 95
Boston MA 45, 58, 88, 105, 106
Boston, H.M.S. 17
Boxer, H.M. Brig 9, 23, 75-83, 85-91,
    93, 94, 96, 99, 100, 107
Boyne 18
Branch 60, 106
Bream, H.M. Schooner 9, 39, 45, 46,
    54, 55-73, 75, 76, 79, 91, 93, 94, 95,
    96, 97, 98
Brenton, Admiral Sir Jahleel 67, 98
Brenton, Captain Edward Pelham 42, 67

Brier Island NS 63, 106
Britt, William 50
Brooks, Anthony 106
Brown, Samuel 50
Brunswicker 9, 31, 42, 43, 44-49, 50,
    51-52, 75, 94, 96. *See also*
    Commodore Barry
Brunswicker, H.M.C.S. 101, 104
Buckskin 39
Buckstown ME 59
Bunker Hill 39
Burrows, Lieutenant William 80, 81,
    83, 86, 88, 99, 101

C

Campobello Island NB 18, 27, 35
Cape Sable NS 38, 39
Cape St. Mary NS 38
Carleton, Governor Thomas 17, 18
Carleton, William 15
Carman, Bliss 21
Carter, A. 108
Carter, J. 108
Castine ME 95, 96, 105
Catherine 38
Charles, William 90
Charlotte County NB 17, 24, 33, 46
Chebacco MA 33
Chesapeake, U.S.S. 24, 27, 56, 76, 77
Chesapeake Bay 56, 98
Chew, Thomas J. 107
Chignecto Isthmus NS 98
Chubb, H.M. Schooner 24
Clausewitz, Karl von 31, 55, 73, 77, 80
Colcord, J. 106
Colibri 38, 39
Collins Jr., T. 107
Colossus, H.M.S. 15
Columbine, H.M. Sloop 27-28
Commodore Barry 30, 39, 40, 41, 42, 43,
    67. *See also Brunswicker*

Concord 35
Confederation 103
Cossack 52
Courtenay Bay NB 96
Cousins, J. 106
Cranberry 59, 60
Cross Jr., J. 107
Crown 64, 65
Curlew 38
Cuttle 18

D

Day, William 48
Deer Island ME 105, 106
Defiance 60, 105
Dipper Harbour NB 46
Disbrow, Noah 96
Discovery 19
Dodge, J. 105
Dolphin 39, 59

E

Earl of Moira 39
Eastern Argus 60
Eastport ME 25, 27-28, 55, 65, 77, 95,
    106
Elbe 35
Elliott, Daniel 41
Emulous, H.M. Brig 38, 52
England. *See* Great Britain
Enterprise, U.S.S. 79-83, 85, 86, 88, 90,
    91, 93, 94, 99, 108

F

Fairplay 23
Fairplay, George 50
Fair Trader 38
Fame 33-35
Fame, The Salem Privateer 33
Federal District Court 78
Filler, Robert 49, 50

Fletcher, Timothy 107, 108
Fly 80
Forester, C.S. 42
Fort Edgecomb ME 64, 65
Fort Preble ME 87
Fort Sullivan ME 31, 95
Fox Island ME 105
Fredericton NB 12, 13, 17
Friendship 38
Frissell, Lieutenant William 22-23

G

Georges Island ME 60, 106
Gleaner 38
Gloucester MA 33
Gossamer 38
Grand Manan NB 33, 35, 52, 98
Great Britain 13, 16, 17, 18, 19, 23, 24,
    25, 26, 27, 29, 35, 44, 47, 56, 69,
    73, 75, 78, 80, 95, 98
Griffith, Edward 98
Gulf of Maine 10, 26, 56, 58, 71, 91,
    94, 95
Gwyn, Julian 23

H

Halifax H.M.S. 27, 39
Halifax NS 17, 18, 19, 21, 22, 27, 28,
    32, 45, 46, 52, 64, 70, 73, 75, 76,
    77, 78, 80, 103
Hardy, Admiral Sir Thomas
    Masterman 67, 95
Hare. See Wasp
Hare, Captain Charles 65-66
Hare, Lieutenant Charles 9, 10, 49,
    65-73, 76, 77, 94, 95, 96, 98, 99,
    103
Hare, Mary Stewart (McGeorge) 69,
    70, 99
Hare, William 99
Harris, M. 107

Harris, W. 107
Hicks, William 50
Hills, Captain George 27-28
Holker 63
Hope 39
Hubley, Martin 27
Hugh, Master's Mate James 23
Hutchinson, James 50

I

impressment 19-24
Increase 64
Indian, H.M.S. 15, 36, 38, 41
Intention 38
Irvin, E.A. 106

J

James, William 56, 57, 91, 99
Jane, Commander Henry 36
Jefferson 60, 106
Jefferson, President Thomas 24, 26, 27
Jennings, Captain 65
John Ward and Sons 98
Johnstone, Hugh 42, 44
Jones, Samuel 50

K

Kennebec ME 106
Kennebec River 78, 79, 81
Kennebunk Beach ME 60
Kennebunk River 62
Kensington PA 80

L

L'Espiral 18
La Solide 18
Lacky, Barnard 50
Laighton, George 23
Lark 60, 105
Lawrence, Captain James 77
Leopard, H.M.S. 24

Lewis 39
Libby, Cyrus 105
Lilly 63
Little River ME 39, 41, 43, 60, 106
Liverpool, Great Britain 98
Longfellow, Henry Wordsworth 100
Loop, D. 105
Lower Canada 16, 17, 22
Loyalists 16, 29, 31, 47, 69, 73
Lubec ME 97
Lukins, H. 106
Lynx, H.M.S. 18

M

Machias ME 95
Madison 35, 39, 41, 42
Madison, President James 24, 90
Madras, H.M.S. 66, 67
Maidstone, H.M.S. 36, 38, 39, 41, 42
Maine Historical Society 63
Manly 95
Margaretta 78, 79, 81
Marryat, Frederick 42, 75, 103
Marshal, L. 105
Martin, H.M. Sloop 95
Maugher's Beach NS 28
McBride, William 50
McCall, Lieutenant Edward 86
McCloud, Donald 72
McCreary, Lieutenant David 86
McCurdy, Robert 50
McDonald, William 50
McFarlane, George 106
McLellan, Captain William 99
McLellan, Stephen 108
McVeal, Alexander 50
McVeal, James 50
Mercer, Keith 22
Merrill Jr., Thomas 99, 107
Merritt, Nehemiah 42, 44

Mills, B. 105
Minerva 17
Minerve, H.M.S. 67
Monhegan ME 58, 59, 60, 79, 88, 105, 106
Montreal QC 95
Moody, Captain Lemuel 82
Moose Island ME 98
Morning Star 38
Morton, R. 107
Mount Desert Island ME 44, 45

N

Napoleonic Wars 24, 75, 98
Nelson, Admiral Horatio 13, 14, 15, 16
Neptune 60, 105
Netherlands 69
Noonan, John 50
Norfolk VA 24
Nova Scotia, H.M. Brig 72

O

O'Brian, Patrick 42, 65
O'Byrne, William 69
Olive 39, 41
Osprey 70

P

Pagan, William 42, 44
Partridge Island NB 96, 97
Passamaquoddy ME 41
Passamaquoddy Bay 22-25, 27, 32, 44, 47, 72, 73, 95
Pattison, Robert 50
Pemaquid Point ME 64, 79, 81
Penobscot ME 105
Penobscot Bay 76
Penobscot River 59, 95
Pictou 21, 95
Pigeon Hill Bay 97

Pilgrim 60, 106
Pincher, H.M. Brig 75
Pleasant River ME 105
Plumper, H.M. Brig 23, 25, 38, 41, 44, 45, 46
Point Lepreau NB 45
Polly 38, 39
Porcupine, H.M.S. 69
Porgey, H.M.S. 24
Portland ME 45, 58, 80, 81, 86-88, 99, 101, 106
Portland Transcript 82
Portsmouth Great Britain 75
Portsmouth NH 80, 105
privateers 10, 32, 33, 39, 41, 42, 43, 44, 45, 52, 55, 58, 61, 78, 80, 91
Prospect ME 106
Pythagoras 54, 105

Q

Quasi-War 80
Quebec, H.M.S. 76
Quincy, J.W. 107
Quoddy Head NB 78

R

Ragged Islands NS 105
Ramillies, H.M.S. 95
Rattler, H.M. Sloop 55, 60, 62, 63
Rattlesnake 108
Reed, Captain James 47, 49, 50, 96, 97
Regulator 39
Reid, James 52
Rice, Mr. 50
Roark, Andrew 49, 50
Robinson, Beverly 46, 47
Rodger, N.A.M. 22, 67, 73, 76, 98
Roosevelt, President Theodore 82
Royal Gazette 31
Royal Marines 41, 42, 71

Royal Navy 9, 13, 16, 17, 18, 19, 22-29, 31, 35, 36, 41, 44, 49, 51, 52, 57, 63, 69, 71, 73, 75, 81, 90, 91, 93, 95, 98, 103
Rutstein, Captain Michael 33, 35

S

Saarlouis Germany 67
Saco ME 105
Sag Harbor NY 41
Saint John NB 13, 15, 17, 18, 22, 23, 24, 25, 28, 33, 34, 35, 42, 44, 45, 46, 47, 49, 51, 52, 53, 59, 63, 65, 69, 70, 71, 72, 73, 75, 76, 78, 79, 91, 93, 94, 95, 96, 97, 98, 99, 103, 104
Salem MA 33, 34, 35, 45, 52, 58, 63, 87, 106
Sally 60, 106
Sawyer, Vice-Admiral Herbert 32, 38
Scott, Charles 50
Scott, Thomas 50
Seal Islands NS 35
Seguin Island ME 59, 60, 62
Semerimes 60, 105
Senhouse, Commodore Henry Le Fleming 9, 95
Shannon, H.M.S. 76
Shelburne 39
Shives, William 23
Smith, George Neilson 12
Smith, Richard 49, 50
Smyley, John 50
Smyth, Governor George Stracey 41, 44, 47, 51
Snap Dragon 96, 104
Spain 69
Spartan, H.M.S. 36, 38, 39, 41, 42, 67
Spence 39
Spring Point ME 81
Spruce 41

Squirrel, H.M. Sloop 25
Stackpole, D. 107
St. Andrews NB 17, 18, 27, 28, 33, 47, 48, 62
Statira 39
Steel, J. 108
St. George NB 17
St. John River 16, 17, 95
St. Lawrence River 17, 22
St. Stephen NB 17
St. Thomas VI 106
Storer, S. 108
Stephens, Lieutenant 21
Sturgis, W. 108
Susannah 60

T

Tappan, Charles 78
Tenedos, H.M.S. 76
Terror, H.M.S. 95
Thrasher, H.M. Brig 75
Townshend 105
Triton 60, 106
Tucker, Captain Samuel 64
Two Brothers 60

U

Union 18
United States 10, 16, 17, 19, 22, 24, 25, 26, 27, 29, 31, 32, 33, 35, 36, 41, 42, 43, 44, 45, 47, 52, 55, 56, 57, 58, 64, 65, 70, 76, 77, 78, 79, 80, 82, 87, 88, 90, 91, 96

Upper Canada 16, 17, 95
US Army 64
US Navy 25, 41, 58, 80, 99

V

Verdun France 67
Vice-Admiralty Court 18, 44, 51, 52, 59, 61, 70, 96, 98
Victory, H.M.S. 66
Vulcan, H.M.S. 65, 66

W

Ward 98
Warren, Admiral Sir John Borlase 18, 70, 95
Washington DC 24, 79
Wasp 63, 80, 96, 106
Waterloo 98
Waters, Midshipman Kerwin 88, 100
Weasel 32, 33
Wells, Frederick 48
West Quoddy Head ME 60, 106
West Quoddy Lighthouse ME 52, 55, 76
Whitten, William 50
William & John 97
Wiscasset ME 64, 65
Wood, Seaman David 72

The New Brunswick Military Heritage Project

The New Brunswick Military Heritage Project, a non-profit organization devoted to public awareness of the remarkable military heritage of the province, is an initiative of the Brigadier Milton F. Gregg, VC, Centre for the Study of War and Society of the University of New Brunswick. The organization consists of museum professionals, teachers, university professors, graduate students, active and retired members of the Canadian Forces, and other historians. We welcome public involvement. People who have ideas for books or information for our database can contact us through our website: www.unb.ca/nbmhp.

One of the main activities of the New Brunswick Military Heritage Project is the publication of the New Brunswick Military Heritage Series with Goose Lane Editions. This series of books is under the direction of J. Brent Wilson, Director of the NBMHP at the University of New Brunswick. Publication of the series is supported by a grant from the Canadian War Museum.

The New Brunswick Military Heritage Series

Volume 1
Saint John Fortifications, 1630-1956,
Roger Sarty and Doug Knight

Volume 2
*Hope Restored: The American Revolution and the Founding
of New Brunswick,* Robert L. Dallison

Volume 3
The Siege of Fort Beauséjour, 1755, Chris M. Hand

Volume 4
*Riding into War: The Memoir of a Horse Transport Driver,
1916-1919,* James Robert Johnston

Volume 5
*The Road to Canada: The Grand Communications Route
from Saint John to Quebec,* W.E. (Gary) Campbell

Volume 6
*Trimming Yankee Sails: Pirates and Privateers
of New Brunswick,* Faye Kert

Volume 7
*War on the Home Front: The Farm Diaries of
Daniel MacMillan, 1914-1927,*
ed. Bill Parenteau and Stephen Dutcher

Volume 8
*Turning Back the Fenians: New Brunswick's
Last Colonial Campaign*, Robert L. Dallison

Volume 9
*D-Day to Carpiquet: The North Shore Regiment
and the Liberation of Europe*, Marc Milner

Volume 10
*Hurricane Pilot: The Wartime Letters
of Harry L. Gill, D.F.M., 1940-1943*,
ed. Brent Wilson with Barbara J. Gill

Volume 11
*The Bitter Harvest of War: New Brunswick and
the Conscription Crisis of 1917*, Andrew Theobald

Volume 12
Captured Hearts: New Brunswick's War Brides,
Melynda Jarratt

Volume 13
*Bamboo Cage: The P.O.W. Diary
of Flight Lieutenant Robert Wyse, 1942-1943*,
ed. Jonathan F. Vance

Volume 14
*Uncle Cy's War: The First World War Letters
of Major Cyrus F. Inches*, ed. Valerie Teed

Volume 15

Agnes Warner and the Nursing Sisters of the Great War,
Shawna M. Quinn

Volume 16

New Brunswick and the Navy: Four Hundred Years,
Marc Milner and Glenn Leonard

About the Author

Joshua M. Smith grew up in the United States on Cape Cod and coastal Maine. He holds degrees from the University of St. Andrews in Scotland, Maine Maritime Academy, East Carolina University, and the University of Maine. From 2001 to 2002 he lived in Ottawa while holding a Fulbright fellowship. He is author of *Borderland Smuggling: Patriots, Loyalists, and Illicit Trade in the Northeast, 1783-1820*, which explores smuggling on the Maine-New Brunswick border and won the John Lyman Award in American Maritime History in 2007. He also edited *Voyages*, a two-volume documents reader in American maritime history produced in conjunction with the National Maritime Historical Society and published in 2009. He currently is an associate professor of Humanities and Director of the American Merchant Marine Museum at the United States Merchant Marine Academy, in Kings Point, New York. Professor Smith lives in New York City with his wife and daughter.

School Board, Water District c

Little interest in other races

By Alex Lear

NORTH YARMOUTH — Enough candidates are on the ballot to create contests in School Board and Yarmouth Water District elections in June, but not for several other town boards.

Incumbent Todd Nicholson of Hawthorne Road, who has served one term, is being challenged for his three-year seat on the School Administrative District 51 Board of Directors by James Moulton of Mill Road, who sat on the board from 2002-2005.

Incumbent Stephen Gorden of Heather Loch, who last year won the District 3 seat on the Cumberland County Commission, i seeking a second term as a Yarmouth Wate District trustee. Guy Watson of Sligo Road who served on the district board from 2006 2009, is running against Gorden.

Incumbent Paul Napolitano is running unopposed for a third, three-year term or the Board of Selectmen. The Mill Ridg Road resident resigned as chairman Apri 3 after the board rejected his attempt to meet in executive session about a survey that sought reaction to the proposed closing of North Yarmouth Memorial School. H believed the survey should have been autho rized by the board before it was published and wanted to discuss the matter in private

Mark Girard of Timber Lane is unop

Election promises changes on Ya

By David Harry

YARMOUTH — While short on contested elections, the June 12 ballot for local offices is long on changes for the Town Council.

Veteran Councilors Carlton Winslow and Erving Bickford did not file to run for new three-year terms, ending a combined 32 years of service on the council.

Councilor Tim Sanders will resign next month with one year left on his term, meaning the seven-member council will have three new members.

David Craig, a current member of the Energy Savers Committee, and Planning Board member James MacLeod filed

nomination papers seeking the two three year terms.

Local real estate agent Pat Thompson i the only candidate to finish Sanders' term.

The School Committee will see some changes, too, with four candidates seeking three seats with three-year terms. Incum bents David Ray, who is the committee chairman, and Craig Wolff are joined on the ballot by Susan Garrett and former Schoo

Celebrating 10 years

Island Treasure

made a splash in War of 1812

COURTESY FREEPORT HISTORICAL SOCIETY

Artist James Lee Berkeley drew this rendering of the Freeport-built Dash, which evaded blockades and captured British ships during the War of 1812. The ship disappeared in a storm in January 1815, according to records at the Freeport Historical Society.

blockaded by British forces. The effects of the war fueled efforts to grant statehood to Maine, which occurred in 1820.

The root causes of the war will be discussed as Smith delves into quarrels between the Americans, British and French regarding free trade and the "impressment" of American sailors to serve on foreign ships.

After the Battle of Baltimore, Americans and other forces defeated the British in the Battle of New Orleans, fought after a peace treaty had been signed in 1815. A month

Comment on this story at:

http://www.theforecaster.net/weblink/121259

before the Treaty of Ghent was signed in February 1815, the Dash disappeared in a gale, possibly off Georges Bank in the Atlantic Ocean.

Admission to the program is $5, with historical society members admitted free.

David Harry can be reached at 781-3661 ext. 110 or dharry@theforecaster.net. Follow David on Twitter: @DavidHarry8.

News briefs